Forgiving as Unity with Christ

DR. ROBERT ENRIGHT

FORGIVING AS UNITY WITH CHRIST

A JOURNEY FOR HEALING RESENTMENT AND RELATIONSHIPS

EWTN Publishing, Inc.
Irondale, Alabama

Cover by LUCAS Art & Design, Jenison, MI

Cover image: *Crucifix by Giotto di Bondone, Church of Ognissanti, Florence (197913745) (c) Rob / stock.adobe.com*

Nihil Obstat: die XXII Maii, anno MMXXIII, John P. Joy, S.T.D.
Censor Librorum

Imprimatur: Madisoniae, die, XXII Maii, anno MMXXIII,
Exc.mus Donaldus Iosephus Hying,
Episcopus Madisonensis

The *Nihil Obstat* and *Imprimatur* are official declarations that a book or pamphlet is free of doctrinal or moral error. No implication is contained therein that those who have granted the *Nihil Obstat* or *Imprimatur* agree with the contents, opinions, or statements expressed.

EWTN Publishing, Inc.
5817 Old Leeds Road, Irondale, AL 35210
Distributed by Sophia Institute Press, Box 5284, Manchester, NH 03108.

paperback ISBN 978-1-68278-427-3
ebook ISBN 978-1-68278-428-0
Library of Congress Control Number: 2024952384

First printing

Contents

BOOK 3

SKEPTICAL VIEWS, SELF-FORGIVENESS,
RESURRECTION JOY, AND YOUR LEGACY

Contents

Foreword

Approximately forty years ago, I was preparing to write a dissertation for my Ph.D. degree. I was unsure of the topic until one Sunday morning, as people were filing out of church after Mass, one of my professors at UW Madison, Professor Robert Enright, asked me how I was doing on my dissertation. My response was negative as I was struggling to acquire the necessary data that were not coming to fruition. He invited me to attend a newly begun not-for-credit seminar on Forgiveness. I did so and that led to my selection of the Forgiveness topic as my dissertation. Over time, this seminar opened the door to the establishment of the International Forgiveness Institute (IFI) with Professor Enright taking the lead. The rest is history. The IFI is now in its thirtieth year, having been formally established in 1994. The IFI now is present in many countries. I feel honored and privileged to have been invited to introduce his latest work on forgiveness which puts words into action.

I have been an ordained Catholic priest for over sixty years, part of which was served as a Chaplain in the Vietnam War during the late 1960s and early 1970s. One of my early assignments was to an air base located on the upper tip of Honshu, the mainland of Japan. At one point during my stay in Japan, I felt, as an American, I had to visit Hiroshima where the first atomic bomb was dropped on August 6, 1945, leading to the end of World War II. I was shocked and devastated as I visited the War Memorial and Museum and observed the devastation of the city and the loss of over 76,000 Japanese lives in one day. Can forgiveness play a part in all that has happened here? I think this experience, as well as my time in Vietnam, together with my extensive counseling experience with parishioners in my Church work opened my heart to doing research on forgiveness with Professor Enright.

Forgiveness is hard work. Even though Christ gave us the two great Commandments of Love of God and Love of Neighbor, He also added a codicil — Love your enemies; pray for those who persecute you (Matthew 5:44). Pope Saint John Paul II once stated, "Forgiving from the heart can sometimes actually be heroic" and then put those words into action when he visited in prison the one who tried to assassinate him, Ali Acha. When asked by a journalist what he said to Acha, John Paul II said, "I forgave as a person." William Barclay, the Protestant clergyman and author, states, "No one can pray for another and still hate the person."

To forgive is one of the greatest gifts we can give one another, whether it be in marriage, within the wider family, or in one's life in the community. If there is to be a mutual, loving relationship in this world through forgiveness it must involve letting go what we are holding in our claw. In a sense forgiveness is the thread that courses through scripture and life. It travels throughout the Old Testament when God proclaimed a year of Jubilee, that all debts were to be forgiven, to the New Testament, be it Peter's denial, the sorrowful thief on the cross, or the Roman crucifixion all encased in the final dying words of Jesus, "Father, forgive them, for they know not what they do" (Luke 23:34). Sadly, our human imperfections often hurt the ones we love the most — a spouse, child, parent, family member, friend, or work associate.

Professor Enright's book details helpful steps we can take as we travel down the road from alienation, to forgiveness, to a possible reconciliation. In a sense we can't heal what we don't feel. If our emotional wounds are ignored, they will fester and over time become worse. We need not only to talk it out but let it out! Often, we see things as we are, not as they are. If the I-glasses we are wearing are filled with hate and bitterness, then our vision is distorted and blurry. Saying the words "I forgive you" and acting on them doesn't mean all is forgotten. Rather it says I want to let go of anger and hate and not only see more clearly but also to work toward respect, trust, and love. It involves taking steps toward being united in love and friendship. Just imagine what it must be like to be that "other person" with whom you are alienated. Using Professor Enright's helpful book, please try to employ forgiveness in your relationships with others. If you hear the other person out and seek reconciliation, then you might make yourself vulnerable when you forgive or even admit you were wrong, but both pay big dividends in the end. Someone must begin the process. Why not you? As someone once said, "The longest journey in the world begins with the first step." Please take to heart and practice in life what Professor Enright has skillfully written here, and you will bring peace within yourself and to others.

Msgr. John Hebl, Oxford, Wisconsin (1935–2024)

Msgr. John Hebl received his doctoral degree in the Department of Counseling Psychology at the University of Wisconsin–Madison. For his doctoral dissertation he did, and published, the very first empirical study of forgiveness therapy. He assisted elderly women to forgive family members who behaved unjustly. The research was published in the American Psychological Association journal Psychotherapy *in 1993.*

Forgiving as Unity with Christ

BOOK ONE

THE PRELIMINARIES AND BASICS OF FORGIVING

CHAPTER 1

The Forgiveness Journey Begins

I am a professor at a university in the United States, a position I have held for over four decades now. I have been studying forgiveness within the social sciences as an academic subject since 1985. I did not always study forgiveness, as I entered academic life in 1977, with an emphasis on the psychology of morals. The popular academic subject in the 1970's was on the theme of justice, particularly on how people come to think, with greater cognitive complexity, about being fair with others. I was an obedient academic, studying, researching, and writing about fairness in the time-honored tradition of such academic luminaries as G. Stanley Hall from the 1890's, Jean Piaget from the 1930's, and Lawrence Kohlberg from the 1960's. Good academics usually are obedient to the spirit of the times whether or not that spirit is uplifting or eventually unimportant.

I awakened one day to ask myself a very dangerous question: Who am I helping with my writing on justice, on how adolescents think about fairness? I concluded that I basically was helping a few of my academic colleagues as we met at professional meetings once or twice a year, patted ourselves on the back for our latest publication, and then went off again to our own research labs, helping no one but ourselves.

At that point, I decided, as I say, to throw all of my publications on justice-thinking over a cliff. I never have gone back to read even one word of those journal articles, even though they were very good to me, offering opportunities for yearly grants and aiding me in securing tenure at a tier-1 university. Upon my abandonment of my path to self-glory, I did not have a new research topic in the area of moral development.

At the time I had just thrown away all of my scholarship on fairness, into my office walked one of my graduate student advisees from Brazil, a serious-minded Catholic. She said that she was out of money, needed a topic for her master's thesis, and would I please give her a research idea. I paused and thought to myself, "Well, this is not the way it works. You are to generate your own idea and then I can help you refine it." Yet, given her difficult monetary situation, I decided to think about her request.

Soon after that, as I was driving alone into the university one day, I decided to pray specifically to Our Heavenly Father for a new topic for our struggling graduate student from Brazil. The mercy of God occurred that day because I was given one and only one word in prayer: forgiveness. "Forgiveness???" This is what I said to myself as I drove the car. I had never, ever thought of that as a topic of research in the social sciences. Thus, this was not coming from me out of my own thought process, but was the mercy of God on me.

So, having received the word "forgiveness" in prayer, within about a week, I walked to the university library and asked the librarian to do a computer search of all of the published scientific studies ever done on the topic of forgiveness. Surely there must be many, given that we all use the word "forgiveness" from time to time. A half hour later, the librarian came back and presented me with a blank sheet of paper. There were no published articles in any of the social sciences that focused specifically on forgiveness research. I then formed a group of graduate students at the university, in 1985, and we formed a not-for-credit seminar that met weekly. We explored three questions: 1) What is forgiveness? 2) How do people go about forgiving? 3) What are the outcomes for people who do forgive?

Little did I know that forgiveness as a research theme in the social sciences would be so controversial. As soon as I started studying forgiveness, a firestorm erupted in academia. My grants dried up. At one point, a professor approached one of my very best graduate students, warning her not to keep working with me because I had ruined my career with such a soft and irrelevant topic as forgiveness in research; she was told that she never would get a job in academia if she continued studying forgiveness. I was scorned when I asked a university to establish an International Forgiveness Institute (and this is why our current International Forgiveness Institute is a private entity). I was told to change the name of my chosen area of study. Call it whatever you wish, but don't call it forgiveness. I learned right away that too much of academia is conformity to the established norms. Step out of line and there will be trouble. Step out of line with one of Jesus Christ's chosen topics, in this case forgiveness, and you are in really big trouble. None of that mattered because my previous study of people's thinking about justice was going to be academic death-through-irrelevance for me. I had to press on with the study of forgiveness.

In the subsequent years, I was able to write three self-help forgiveness books for the general public, engage in forgiveness counseling because of my psychologist's license, and write two forgiveness books for mental health professionals. Yet, none of them presents the richness and depth of forgiveness as this current book does.

This book is the mature fruit of what happened through grace in 1985. Everything in Books Two and Three here was hidden from me early in the exploration of forgiveness. It was not until I became what they call a "revert" to the Catholic faith that the depth, richness, and genuine beauty of forgiveness came to me. My pursuit of the topic of forgiveness played a large part in this reverting back to my childhood faith, given to me by my parents.

What you are about to read in this book all emerged because of Our Heavenly Father's mercy on me on that day in 1985 and because of the insights on unity with Christ that come from Catholicism. What you are about to read in this book, I cannot take the credit as that credit belongs to Our Heavenly Father, Jesus Christ's Crosswork, and the revelations within the Catholic Church. I am a temporary messenger for what forgiveness truly is. The eternal message belongs to God and His eternal Catholic Church.

A Primary Motivation for Writing This Book

It has been my great honor to give forgiveness retreats and talks for the Missionaries of Charity in Edinburgh, Scotland and Rome, Italy. After a retreat in Edinburgh in January 2020, a sister looked at me and said, "Don't you ever quit giving these retreats! Don't you ever quit!"

Well … The next month came the global pandemic and I was not able to return to give already-scheduled retreats for the sisters in London and in Northern Italy. I only now am starting my talks again with the sisters. So, what am I to do so that I "do not quit"? The answer is this little book, which I hope to present to the Missionaries' houses in which the sisters request it. This is my way of continuing the journey begun by invitation from them. This book is written not only for the Missionaries of Charity but also for all people who want to draw closer to Jesus Christ in the context of being wounded by others' transgressions against them. As people engage in the exercises within this book not only may their broken hearts be healed but also may they realize that their hearts are enlivened toward a deeper relationship with Jesus with an awakening to the profound importance of the Catholic faith and the Catholic Church.

This is not my written attempt to give a retreat. This little book is much different than a retreat in at least three ways. First, it is not meant to last for only three days, as the retreats have lasted. Instead, the exercises in this book will take contemplation and time.

Second, there is journaling and so those engaging with the reflections in this book will be creating their own written history to look back and see the progress that has been made. You may find that you are maturing as you walk this path of forgiving with me and as you reflect in writing as I ask you questions at different stops along the pathway. Further, you can go back and reflect in more depth on information that you encountered days, weeks, or months ago and continue to explore that which is important to you.

Third, this is not at all meant to be a one-time road trip of forgiveness, but instead a journey that you, as the reader and participant in the exercises, will travel again and again with different people in mind to forgive. Think of this book as a life's companion as you grow more deeply in the mystery and majesty of forgiving.

The book is divided into what I call three books, with deference to Thomas a Kempis' approach in his Late Medieval masterpiece, *The Imitation of Christ*. He divided his reflections into short chapters within four books. We do the same here, within three books and short chapters in each. In the first book, we look at what it means to forgive in a basic way, more general than the Catholic perspective. We examine the biblical stories of Joseph forgiving his half-brothers in Genesis and the Prodigal Son in Luke's Gospel. We look at common definitions of forgiveness and a pathway to forgiving.

This sets the stage for Book 2 which is the decidedly Catholic perspective. It comes from as deep a Catholic perspective as I am able to see. The Catholic perspective, as I have studied it, practiced it, and taught it, is the most beautiful approach to forgiving others that I have ever seen. Catholic forgiving is one major reason why I am a Catholic. As you will see, the Catholic approach to forgiving is an intimate and loving connection with Jesus Christ for those who have hurt you. There is nothing else like it in the world. In Book 2 also is a section on seeking forgiveness from others.

Book 3 starts with an examination of skeptical views of forgiveness and of Christianity. I discuss these to strengthen you as others will be criticizing you as you practice forgiveness and as you practice your Catholic faith. It is important that you stand strong in the face of opposition. We then focus on forgiving yourself, forgiveness within community, the joy of the forgiveness resurrection, and the challenging issue of what will be your legacy in this world when you pass on.

Again in deference to Thomas a Kempis, we have numbered many of the paragraphs or sections within each chapter of each book. This is done to emphasize that each numbered section is a thought unto itself and can be used for reflection and entries into your journal. Because I will be asking you throughout this forgiveness journey to do some written reflections in your private journal, please have paper and a writing instrument, or your trusty computer for word processing, ready at the end of some of the sections.

Finally, this is not a book in which I primarily tell you about forgiveness. Instead, it is a book in which you are encouraged to experience forgiveness and to do so intimately with Jesus Christ. Pope Benedict XVI (Ratzinger, 2002), in his message to a meeting of the ecclesial movement Communion and Liberation, made the important distinction between knowing beauty through formal education and direct experience from the heart. The latter, he said, we need to rediscover as a central need of our time. Your exercises from the heart in this book represent this kind of experiential learning that you are encouraged to embrace and then communicate to others.

May those of you on this journey of forgiveness be as blessed as I have been in writing it.

CHAPTER 2

Our Loving Heavenly Father

THE GRACE OF GOD is transformative. A broken heart can be transformed to a mended heart when we have been treated badly by others. For this to happen, we have to cooperate with that grace, surrender to that grace so that God can provide all that is needed for healing. A major part of healing from injustices against us is to reawaken or to deepen the love within us. For this healing to happen by grace, we are asked to walk a pathway of forgiveness.

The point of this book is to show you this pathway so that you can go from a broken heart to a mended heart, joyful "with Jesus, for Jesus, and to Jesus" (Mother Teresa, 1985, pg. 97). You will not walk this pathway alone, but with Jesus and His grace. The pathway is difficult because forgiveness occurs in the face of betrayal, disrespect, abandonment, and other sometimes surprising acts of injustice against us, often by those people who are to love us the most. We need strength to walk this difficult path. That strength starts and ends with God's love for us, through His merciful grace. Therefore, let us start our forgiveness journey by reflecting on Who God is.

1. Let us begin by quietly reflecting on the theme that God is Love. Please read and think about each Bible verse below from the Old Testament. (The Bible verses are from the Revised Standard Version. The RSV was chosen because of

its fidelity to the original languages in both the Old and New Testaments.)

> *Deuteronomy 7:9: Know therefore that the Lord your God is God, the faithful God who keeps covenant and steadfast love with those who love him and keep his commandments, to a thousand generations.*
>
> *Psalm 136:26: O give thanks to the God of heaven, for his steadfast love endures for ever.*
>
> *Jeremiah 31:3: I have loved you with an everlasting love; therefore I have continued my faithfulness to you.*

JOURNAL REFLECTION: Consider these adjectives and verbs as you reflect on the intensity of God's love for you: *steadfast, endures,* and *everlasting.*

2. Please now reflect on these nine Bible verses from the New Testament.

> *1 John 3:1: See what love the Father has given us, that we should be called children of God; and so we are. The reason why the world does not know us is that it did not know him.*
>
> *1 John 4:7: Beloved, let us love one another; for love is of God, and he who loves is born of God and knows God.*
>
> *1 John 4:8: God is love.*

1 John 4:16: So we know and believe the love God has for us. God is love, and he who abides in love abides in God, and God abides in him.

1 John 4:18: There is no fear in love, but perfect love casts out fear. For fear has to do with punishment, and he who fears is not perfected in love.

1 John 4:19: We love, because he first loved us.

John 3:16: For God so loved the world that he gave his only Son, that whoever believes in him should not perish but have eternal life.

John 15:13: Greater love has no man than this, that a man lay down his life for his friends.

Romans 5:8: But God shows his love for us in that while we were yet sinners Christ died for us.

JOURNAL REFLECTION: How great is God's love for you; what is the biblical evidence above of the greatness of this love? What does it mean to be a "child of God"? When we love others, are we loving those who are children of God? Are all people children of God?

3. Who is God? Please think of one time in which you, personally, experienced the unconditional love of God. My encounter with Him and His mercy in the car that day, when receiving the one word "forgiveness," is one of my own examples.

> **JOURNAL REFLECTION:** Try to write down some of the specifics of this one experience so that it becomes very present to you now.

4. Now please take some time to quietly reflect on one situation you have experienced in which one person in your life showed you unconditional love. Maybe it was a parent when you were a small child. Perhaps it was a teacher or a friend or a mentor when you were struggling. Try to reconstruct this person and the event in your mind, heart, and soul. Try to re-experience the unconditional love so that this love is present now to you. *my parents*

> **JOURNAL REFLECTION:** Write down this concrete experience of love so that you can return to it later as you engage in the exercises within this book.

5. Try now to remember these visits of love and please try to keep them in your heart as you start the forgiveness journey. As you are loved, and have concretely experienced that love, you will be asked to extend the love in your heart to others, to those who were not loving you when they acted unfairly.

CHAPTER 3

"Father, Forgive Them"

THE PURPOSE OF THIS reflection is to think about Jesus' forgiveness first, before we start to think about forgiving those who have wounded us. Consider this vital verse:

> *Luke 23:34: Father, forgive them, for they know not what they do.*

1. I would like to make six points about this verse and then add a seventh idea for you: The context is the brutal Crucifixion. The Roman soldiers expected crying out, cursing, and even blasphemy. Cicero reported that at times the soldiers would cut out the tongues of the crucified ones to prevent further blasphemy. Jesus, in contrast, proclaimed forgiveness.

2. As the Venerable Servant of God Archbishop Fulton Sheen (1952) states, Jesus used the words "for they know not what they do" because if they knew that they were crucifying God, the second Person of the Trinity, then they would be turning completely from God, jeopardizing their salvation. Of course, because there is no limit to God's saving power, they still may have been redeemed to salvation.

3. Why did not Jesus Himself say, "I forgive you"? Why did He then ask the Father to do so? He was showing that at that

moment He was the sacrifice. As the sacrifice, He was humbling Himself. Even though He was the sacrifice, He was in charge on the Cross: "No one takes it [life] from me, but I lay it down of my own accord" (John 10:18).

4. The proclamation of forgiveness under the most dire of circumstances — a cruel murder — continued to be echoed short years later when Stephen proclaimed forgiveness for the ones who murdered him: "As they were stoning Stephen, he prayed, 'Lord Jesus, receive my spirit.' And he knelt down and cried with a loud voice, 'Lord, do not hold this sin against them.' And when he had said this, he fell asleep" (Acts 7:59–60).

5. St. Paul did the same under deep injustice when he proclaimed in 2 Timothy 4:16: "All deserted me. May it not be charged against them."

6. It is now our turn to bring this kind of person-to-person forgiveness forward in time to today, to our hurts, for those who wound us.

7. Your forgiving is so important, so powerful that it can destroy evil. Consider this quotation from Pope Benedict XVI during his Pentecost Sunday sermon in Roma, 2005:

> Evil can be overcome only by forgiveness. Certainly, it must be an effective forgiveness; but only the Lord can give us this forgiveness, a forgiveness that drives away evil not only with words but truly destroys it. Only suffering can bring this about and it has truly taken place with the suffering love of Christ, from whom we draw the power to forgive.

JOURNAL REFLECTIONS: From the passages above, Who is Jesus? Please reflect on the fact that He is the Suffering Servant of Isaiah 53, verse 5: "But he was wounded for our transgressions, he was bruised for our iniquities; upon him was the chastisement that made us whole, and with his stripes we are healed."; verses 10b and 11: "when he makes himself an offering for sin, he shall see his offspring, he shall prolong his days; the will of the LORD shall prosper in his hand; he shall see the fruit of the travail of his soul and be satisfied; by his knowledge shall the righteous one, my servant, make many to be accounted righteous; and he shall bear their iniquities."

What is forgiveness from the vantage point of Jesus dying on the Cross for you?

CHAPTER 4

Before Forgiving: Pride vs. Humility

1. When people are hurt by others, it is not at all uncommon to hear, "How dare you!" or "I will get even," or "Revenge is mine." An academic who studies forgiveness recently said to me, "Forgiveness used to be popular, but no more in our society that is getting more contentious."

2. An initial response of indignation is good because it shows you that you are a person of worth and should be treated with respect. Yet, too often we cling to resentment because of pride. Pride within each one of us seems to be part of the fallen nature. So, there is a war going on within each of us between the fallen nature and human nature restored and elevated (or divinized) by grace. Reflect for a moment on this war as brought out in scripture: Romans 7:23–25 states, "But I see in my members another law at war with the law of my mind and making me captive to the law of sin which dwells in my members. Wretched man that I am! Who will deliver me from this body of death? Thanks be to God through Jesus Christ our Lord! So then, I of myself serve the law of God with my mind, but with my flesh I serve the law of sin."

JOURNAL REFLECTION: Do you see the fallen nature within you and, at the same time, see the way out of that, by "the law of God"? *Yes*

3. A significant part of winning against this "law of sin" is to practice the moral virtue of humility. Please take some time to reflect on the importance of humility in these Bible verses:

> Psalm 25:8–9: Good and upright is the LORD;
> therefore he instructs sinners in the way.
> He leads the humble in what is right, and
> teaches the humble his way.

> Proverbs 16:5: Every one who is arrogant is
> an abomination to the LORD; be assured, he
> will not go unpunished.

> Proverbs 29:23: A man's pride will bring him
> low, but he who is lowly in spirit will obtain
> honor.

> Micah 6:8: He has showed you, O man, what
> is good; and what does the Lord require of
> you but to do justice, and to love kindness,
> and to walk humbly with your God?

> Proverbs 29:23: A man's pride will bring him
> low, but he who is lowly in spirit will obtain
> honor.

> Matthew 11:29–30: Take my yoke upon you,
> and learn from me; for I am gentle and lowly
> in heart, and you will find rest for your souls.
> For my yoke is easy, and my burden is light.

Ephesians 4:2: With all lowliness and meekness, with patience, forbearing one another in love.

Philippians 2:3: Do nothing from selfishness or conceit, but in humility count others better than yourselves.

1 Corinthians 1:28–29: God chose what is low and despised in the world, even things that are not, to bring to nothing things that are, so that no human being might boast in the presence of God.

James 4:10: Humble yourselves before the Lord and he will exalt you.

Luke 18:11–12: The Pharisee stood and prayed thus with himself, "God, I thank thee that I am not like other men, extortioners, unjust, adulterers, or even like this tax collector. I fast twice a week, I give tithes of all that I get."

JOURNAL REFLECTIONS: Are you a sinner in need of Jesus' grace? Do you share a sin nature with those who have sinned against God and who were unfair to you?

How would you define humility in light of the Bible verses above?

How can you practice humility? One example: Go to Eucharistic Adoration and reflect on two dimensions of Jesus Christ: 1) He is the Lord of the universe and will come again in power and majesty, and 2) He is loving you as He is in the form of lowly unleavened bread. See Him in His lowly state within the Eucharist. How can you practice humility now?

If you want to be like Jesus, how can you be like Him in His state of unleavened bread?

Do you get an overall sense of what it means to be humble as you reflect on Jesus Christ in His state of unleavened bread? How would you describe what humility is and its value now?

Can you bring this sense of humility with you as we explore what forgiving others is?

4. It is important not to grow discouraged that you are a sinner who sometimes displeases God. Let us go back to Book 1, Chapter 2 and reflect on God's love for you. Keep this fact in your heart as we proceed.

JOURNAL REFLECTION: Can you see God's unconditional love for you as a person?

CHAPTER 5

Some Preliminary Lessons on Forgiveness

1. Here is a working definition of forgiving, including what
    forgiveness is not:

    When we forgive, we are good to those who are not good
    to us; we are trying to love those who are not loving us.
    Forgiveness is: a) in the context of being treated unjustly by
    others; b) a deliberate attempt to give up resentment toward
    that person; and c) the deliberate striving toward offering
    kindness, respect, generosity, and love to that person.

    Forgiveness is under the banner of *agape* or charity, or
    giving to others for their sake. This *agape* can be difficult
    and painful for the one who loves. This is why forgiving is so
    heroic.

    Forgiveness is not: a) Condoning or excusing the injustice
    done. That injustice was, is, and always will be wrong;
    b) Forgetting. We do not forget atrocities against us. We tend
    to remember in new ways, without rancor or hatred toward
    the one who was unjust; c) Reconciliation. Reconciliation is
    a negotiation strategy between two or more people trying to
    make their way back to each other in mutual trust. Forgive-
    ness, in contrast, is a moral virtue which you can practice
    even if the other is unwilling to explore the possibility of

reconciliation with you; d) Abandoning the quest for justice. When someone makes a snide comment about you when you talk to each other, you can forgive the person and ask for more civility in the conversation; and e) A sign of weakness. It takes courage to bear the pain of what happened, a strong will to persevere in the forgiving, wisdom to know how to forgive, and moderation so that one's anger is in control before it is reduced.

2. The Lord's Prayer/Our Father

Please slowly recite the Our Father. Notice two insights: First notice how often the words "our," "us," and "we" appear (nine times in this one short prayer). We are in this together, as a community of believers and forgivers. Second, which phrase is the longest in the entire prayer? It is the exhortation to forgive: "Forgive us our trespasses as we forgive those who trespass against us" (twelve words). Even the opening praise to the Father is only ten words. Even the request for the kingdom to come (three words) and Thy will to be done (eleven words) are shorter than the exhortation to forgive. Even the deliverance petition at the end is only four words. Forgiving and being forgiven is given the most space in this most important prayer.

3. Let us now examine Jesus' one and only recorded commentary on the Lord's Prayer in Matthew 6:14–15, which is this: "For if you forgive men their trespasses, your heavenly Father also will forgive you; but if you do not forgive men their trespasses, neither will your Father forgive your trespasses." Our first lesson on forgiving from this passage from Matthew's Gospel is this: Notice that Jesus did not focus on the word "hallowed" or on our daily bread. He focused only

on forgiveness from that important prayer. Forgiving must be very important to Jesus for Him to do that.

> **JOURNAL REFLECTION:** Given that Jesus could have given us many other ideas in the Lord's Prayer and given that His one and only one commentary on this prayer concerned our forgiving others, how important to Jesus is your forgiving of others? Why do you think your forgiving is so important to Him?

4. As a second lesson from the Lord's Prayer, forgiving is in the larger context of being forgiven. This is further described by Pope Benedict XVI in his book *Jesus of Nazareth* (Ratzinger, 2007, p. 85):

> Enmity with God is the source of all that poisons Man; overcoming this enmity is the basic condition for peace in the world. Only the man who is reconciled with God can also be reconciled and in harmony with himself, and only the man who is reconciled with God and with himself can establish peace around him and throughout the world.

In other words, we first need to be in the state of grace with our Heavenly Father. This puts us in harmony with ourselves. It is then that we can do the fruitful work of forgiving others.

– re: W. Federer
very offended

5. Forgiving and Natural Law
    Hebrew (*salah*), Christian (*aphiemi*), ~~Muslim (*afo*)~~, Confucian (*shu*), Hindu, and Buddhist perspectives all make room for forgiveness and see it as a morally worthwhile activity. In

fact, I have never read an ancient text with a moral basis to it that did not value forgiveness. Forgiveness cuts across many different philosophies and religions. It is "written on the heart."

JOURNAL REFLECTION: What is the relationship between your going to the Sacrament of Confession and your forgiving others? What is the relationship between how you understand forgiving and how others who have hurt you might understand forgiving?

CHAPTER 6

Forgiving from the Bible Stories

1. The oldest preserved accounts of forgiveness, from any source as far as I can tell, are within the Old Testament. An important example is Joseph, who unconditionally forgives his half-brothers in Genesis 37–45. Joseph was the favored son of Jacob. This engendered jealousy in the half-brothers, who plotted his demise. They threw him down a well to murder him, changed their minds, and instead of dusting him off and saying, "Welcome back into the family," they sold him into slavery in Egypt. In Egypt he was imprisoned and eventually he interpreted a dream of the pharaoh, gaining esteem. He was exalted to a governorship. One day, here come all of his half-brothers to Egypt, asking for help in averting a famine in the land of the Hebrews. Joseph recognized his relatives; they did not recognize him. After all, they would never have suspected that Joseph had risen out of slavery to a powerful governmental position. Was he forgiving? We cannot be sure what was in his heart by his action of throwing all of them into prison. Was he angry and his motive revenge? Was he trying to lead them to repentance, as the *Haydock Catholic Bible Commentary* (Haydock, 2018/1811) suggests? We are not sure because the Bible does not describe his inner world.

When Joseph heard them lamenting their fate in prison (they were blaming their current fate on their abuse of Joseph years ago), he wept. Joseph decided that he wanted to see his full-brother, Benjamin, who did not accompany the others to Egypt. So, he commanded the half-brothers to leave Egypt and bring Benjamin back to Egypt with them. He still did not reveal himself as Joseph or say that Benjamin was his brother. To assure their future arrival, he kept Simeon in prison, saying that he will not be released unless they return with Benjamin.

When they returned and he saw Benjamin, Joseph wept for a second time. Was this his moment of forgiving, as demonstrated by acts of mercy? It does not seem like it, because once he lavished sufficient goods to save the Hebrew nation from famine, he played a trick on them. He hid a silver goblet in Benjamin's knapsack. When they were almost out of Egypt, Joseph, with an army of soldiers, overtook the caravan, pulled the silver goblet out of Benjamin's knapsack, accused him of theft, and demanded Benjamin's arrest.

At that point, Judah tore his own garment, and in an act of self-sacrifice, asked that he be taken instead of Benjamin, as a way of sparing the father Jacob's angst in learning that he will never see Benjamin again. At that point of self-sacrifice on the part of Judah, Joseph wept a third time. This is a significant moment because the number three is a sign of perfection in the Bible (the Holy Trinity being one example; Jesus being in the grave for three days being a second example). Joseph then revealed himself as Joseph and embraced his relatives in a genuine act of forgiveness. His forgiveness allowed them to continue with the caravan of provisions back to the Hebrew nation.

Our lessons regarding forgiveness from this ancient story are these. First, Joseph's forgiving helped to save the Hebrew nation. This is how powerful forgiving can be. Without Joseph's forgiveness as part of God's plan, the Hebrew nation would have been in big trouble because of the famine. Second, if Joseph was angry, and again we cannot be sure, this anger, as a response to injustice, can give the message "I am a person who deserves respect." Third, forgiving is not a simple, straight line from resentment to full forgiveness. Notice that Joseph went back and forth from imprisoning his relatives, then to weeping, then to playing a trick on them, and then more weeping, before he embraced his relatives and finally let them be on their way. Fourth, upon forgiving, the forgiver begins to see the one who offended in a different way. Joseph, in lavishing the provision on them and embracing them through his tears, certainly seemed to see his relatives as persons, far beyond their offenses against him. Fifth, his feelings at the end of the story showed a softness toward the relatives, including compassion for them. Compassion is a willingness to suffer along with others. Sixth, his forgiving included behavior, which is not always the case if, for example, someone abandons the forgiver or the one who offends is deceased. Yet, in Joseph's case, the behavior was an abundant gift-giving of food and animals to avert a famine. Seventh, please notice that Joseph's forgiving was unconditional in that he never waited for an apology prior to his forgiving. After all, how could they repent with an apology when the half-brothers did not even know this was Joseph?

2. The New Testament and forgiving follow in this same tradition. The Koine Greek words for forgiving are *aphiemi* (to forgive; a quality relationship is restored between God and the formerly sinful person) and *agape* (love that includes suffering directly for particular persons; creative, forgiving love).

3. The Prodigal Son (Luke 15:11–32) follows in the tradition
of Joseph. Here we have a Hebrew son who behaved badly,
asking his father for his inheritance before the father was
deceased. The son then left the farm, squandered the money,
and became so destitute that he began to work on a pig farm,
which is not a very good thing for a Hebrew boy to do. He
sank so low that he said to himself that he would return to his
father and ask if he could be a hired hand on the farm. Notice
that the father, if he is an earthly father and not only a symbol
of Our Heavenly Father, would not have heard this repentance.

When the prodigal son reached his father's land, his father
saw him from afar. The father, of course, did not know why his
son was returning. Perhaps he was returning to ask for more
money or to get his laundry done. Nonetheless, the father ran to
his son and embraced him, as Joseph did with his half-brothers,
before the son could apologize or say why he was there.

The father forgave his son unconditionally. The father
lavished love on his son, killing the fatted calf, celebrating
the return of his son. The older brother took offense at this
outpouring of generosity, as can happen when other family
members see people forgiving, with great love, those who dis-
rupted that family. As the father explained to the older brother,
everything here has been yours (for the older brother), but his
younger brother was lost and now is found. Forgiveness can
help restore a family to true community.

History here is our teacher as we see that forgiving is
reaching out in our pain to those who caused the pain. To forgive is to reach out with love, in your pain, to the one toward
whom you might have been harboring resentment, perhaps
even for years. Do you see why forgiveness is controversial?
How outrageous is this: to reach out with great love to those

who were cruel? It does not make sense to the mind trained on secular philosophies, toward secular pursuits. After all, should not we be standing firm, demanding justice, letting offenders know that they must pay for what they did? Forgiveness, in contrast, extends the hand of mercy and says to the other, "Come, take my hand and come out of the pit."

We thus have similar insights from the story of the Prodigal Son as we received from Joseph's story. We do not know if the father was angry, because the story does not say, but we certainly can imagine that the father was carrying pain for a long time because of his son's actions. He does think of his son as precious, as a genuine special person, not because of what he did, but in spite of those actions. His feelings include compassion and his behavior includes an abundant giving. As with Joseph, the father forgives unconditionally, not waiting for the son to first apologize.

JOURNAL REFLECTION: So, then, what is forgiveness in a person-to-person sense? Take some time in your journal to reflect on your understanding, at this point, of what forgiving another person actually is.

CHAPTER 7

What Is Forgiveness?

Let us now take some time to reflect on what forgiving another person actually is, what it is not, and some reasons for forgiving those who hurt us. There are eight points for your consideration.

1. What does forgiveness have in common with: justice, courage, patience, and kindness? All of these are moral virtues.

   What is a moral virtue? A moral virtue concerns goodness toward the welfare of persons, and this includes others and the self. It originates inside a person as the will to good and is expressed as a good to others. The *Catechism of the Catholic Church*, in paragraph 1803, states: "A virtue is an habitual and firm disposition to do the good. It allows the person not only to perform good acts, but to give the best of himself. The virtuous person tends toward the good with all his sensory and spiritual powers; he pursues the good and chooses it in concrete actions."

   Justice is one of the clearest examples of a moral virtue benefitting others and the self. For example, if Person A contracts with Person B to build a table, then the agreed-upon exchange of funds for the table shows mutual benefit. While being prudent, temperate, and courageous all may help the self grow in character, those virtues benefit others as well. For example, an intemperate gambler who becomes temperate in his betting now benefits the family and the family's finances. A courageous soldier, by marching into and winning the battle, benefits the countrymen. A wise teacher knows what to teach a child, how to do this, and when to do it, thus benefitting the student.

The moral virtue of forgiveness is part of the moral virtue of mercy and mercy is part of the more-encompassing moral virtue of *agape* love. *Agape* love is in service to others and can be sacrificial as the person gives to others even when it is inconvenient to do so.

2. What is forgiveness?

Formal definition: *In essence, we can say that forgiveness is a moral virtue, unconditionally expressed as an act of mercy toward those who have acted unjustly toward the forgiver.*

3. What is forgiveness?

How does forgiveness differ from "letting it go," "moving on," excusing, or reconciling?

Forgiveness differs from these concepts because none of them are moral virtues. For example, one can "let it go" because the person thinks the offending person is a little less than human, and therefore he is dismissed. As another example, reconciliation does not originate inside one person as the will to good, but instead is a *negotiation between two or more people for the purpose of mutual harmony in a relationship.* One can forgive without reconciling, but one cannot be said to be forgiving if the motive is to dismiss the person as a person.

4. What is forgiveness?

We need to make a distinction between the *natural virtues* and the *infused virtues* (grace from the Holy Spirit). Is forgiveness a natural or an infused virtue? Could it be both, with its perfection coming as an infused virtue?

5. What is forgiveness?

    Is forgiveness a skill, a coping strategy, or even a commitment? How might forgiveness differ from these?

    A complete moral virtue concerns *understanding* (at least to a degree) of the good, *motivation* to do the good (I desire to do this), *the will to effect a good action* (I definitely will do it), the *commitment* to focus that will (I will do it in a particular way with a particular plan), and the *behaviors to fulfill the internal transformations* toward the good.

6. What is the difference between *forgiving someone* and *being a forgiving person*?

    Forgiving someone can be a one-time act. *Being a forgiving person* means that you live a life of forgiveness, where it is close to you, important to you, an important part of your life.

7. Why should I forgive? What is my goal in forgiving?

    I'm hurting and need some relief.

    The other who offended me is hurting and needs some relief, especially so that he or she grows in the moral virtues (such as patience, kindness, and love).

    The forgiving makes possible a uniting in moral love with an offending other or others, if the other is willing to truly reconcile.

    The practice of any virtue, including forgiveness, is good in and of itself regardless of what follows from its expression.

    Jesus Christ commands it. Is this good because Jesus commands it (Divine Command theory) or does Jesus command it because it is good and rational (part of Natural Law, part of Who Jesus is)?

    I want to imitate Jesus and do as He has done.

I want to unite with Jesus. I want a deeper relationship with Jesus and I can have that as I forgive those who have hurt me.

8. Why should I forgive? — and one practical point to consider.

As one practical point, I was in the Philippines in 2019 and as part of a series of talks, I addressed a group of people who assist priests in the process of exorcism. One large preparatory part, prior to the actual exorcism, is helping the person who is oppressed or possessed to forgive those who have been deeply unfair to him or her. If the person does not forgive, I was told, then this can hinder the efficacy of the exorcism. This is one practical lesson within the Catholic faith of just how important it is to forgive those who have hurt us in a serious say. From their own practical experience, those in the Philippines inform us that forgiving or not forgiving both have a profound influence on our spiritual life. ✓

JOURNAL REFLECTION: Before you examine the road map of forgiving, what are the key insights you have from this chapter that might help you to better understand what forgiveness is and some of the goals of forgiving at this point in your journey?

CHAPTER 8

A Process Model or Road Map
of How People Forgive

Before we go on our first forgiveness journey together, let us pause and open our road map so that we can see where we are going. The particular road map is what I call the Process Model of Forgiveness, pieced together by examining how others have forgiven in the past and who have described at least part of their forgiveness journey in print. It was further pieced together by describing this process to hundreds of people and asking for their opinions about how they, personally, have forgiven those who have hurt them. Our research team then did extensive scientific studies, described in the next chapter, to validate this road map, to see if it is valid, to see if it works with a wide variety of people suffering from many different kinds of injustices. Come with me, then, and let us open the map as I describe this one road to forgiving.

1. How Do I Forgive? A General Summary

   Here then is the pathway to forgiving, the Process Model of Forgiveness, which has four phases and 20 units across these four phases. All of this is outlined in Table 1 below.

2. The first phase, which we call the *Uncovering Phase*, is for you to simply acknowledge that you have been treated unfairly and

then to quietly reflect on the *effects* of that injustice for you. Did you know that most people are unaware of how injustices against them actually affect them? They do not connect what happened to them ten years ago with their restless sleep now, or their fatigue now, or even their leaving God and the Church. One of the biggest questions people have is, "Why would God allow evil?" When they do not come up with a very good answer because their hearts are broken, they think they are doing themselves a favor by leaving the Faith. That is exactly what evil wants from them rather than unity. When we talk with people who have been treated very unjustly and we see this kind of pessimism, we also see this development of a negative worldview, that no one can be trusted, that there is little hope in the world. We see anger at God.

At times, a person can obsess about the injustice and this obsession is another effect that can last for years. I talked with one young man, a college student, who told me that when he was a child, his father used to beat him frequently. Now as a college student, every night when he went to bed, he would have a dream of his father chasing him. Every night, he knew what his dreams would be. He forgave his father and the dream left. Do you see that he was haunted by what happened fifteen years ago? He left home, was living in a dormitory at the university, but he had not run away from the injustice. It was still in his heart, mind, and soul. It was only through forgiving that the *effects* of the continual injustices ceased.

Thus, Phase One is to courageously examine the effects of the injustices against you. Do you know what one of these effects is? It is not having the will to stand up straight, not having the will to bear the pain, and get a job or to do God's will. One of the effects over time tends to be not taking care of oneself or others. Thank you, Missionaries of Charity, for taking care of the poor, some of whom are struggling to take care of themselves. Many of them are crushed by the past injustices against them and they do not even know this. I talked recently with one person on the Royal Mile in Edinburgh, Scotland. He was sitting against a wall with a tin cup near him. I asked him, "What injustices have you suffered?" He said, "None. I never have had an injustice against me." Yet, his face was tortured. The pain on his face was obvious, but he may have been in denial. He was not ready to even look at any injustices against him. I suspect that if I had a week with him, those injustices against him would come pouring out. For now, he is sitting there, not knowing why he is there, leaning against the wall, relying on the generosity of others for his daily sustenance. This is what I mean by the *effects* of injustice and the effects of the injustice can be poisonous. So, when people finally realize that there is a poison that happens after being treated unjustly, they become motivated to address it. The poison does vary across people. For example, some people ruminate about the injustice, as the college student was doing in his incessant dreams about his father. Others are chronically fatigued. Some have a little poison inside while others are steeped in the poison, to such an extent that it literally kills them. Darrell

3. We then ask this, which is the beginning of Phase Two of Four, the Decision Phase: "Are you willing to try forgiveness as a ✓ solution to the effects of the poison abiding within you as a result of being treated unjustly?" By then, most people say yes because they have new insight into their inner pain which they have been carrying. They know that they have to do something about this pain, this poison, especially if what they have tried up

to this point has not worked to reduce or eliminate it. Then we go through the definition of forgiveness. We say: "You will be trying to do good to those who have not been good to you. You will be deliberately trying to get rid of resentment and offering goodness of some kind toward the one who hurt you. This is a form of mercy; it is a form of love. You will not be excusing the other's behavior. You will not be forgetting or automatically reconciling or abandoning a quest for justice. Do you want to do this?" If the person agrees, then we go to the third of four phases in the Process Model of Forgiveness.

4. Phase Three is called the Work Phase. This is where we really roll up our forgiveness sleeves and ask the forgivers what we call *thinking questions* first about the one who hurt them. We ask questions in three categories, what we call the Personal Perspective, the Global Perspective, and the Cosmic Perspective. The Personal Perspective is to try and see the vulnerability, the weaknesses, the difficulties, the emotional wounds in the one who wounded the forgiver. In all likelihood, the person who acted unjustly is carrying a lot of wounds because wounded people wound other people. Thus, we ask the person who is forgiving to think about the history of woundedness within the person who wounded him or her.

    In the vast majority of cases, and sadly, those who hurt us the most are the ones we know the most. Oftentimes, it is family members who have wounded us. If someone were robbed at the Piazza Navona in Roma by someone wearing a mask, then the forgiver will not know the personal history of the one who pointed the gun and took the money. In this case, we would skip the Personal Perspective and go to the Global Perspective. Yet, most of the time we can engage the forgiver in the Personal Perspective. So you see the vulnerabilities, you see the weaknesses, you see the fears in the other. You see the brokenness in the other, not to excuse, not to necessarily automatically reconcile, not to throw away justice, but to see the truth in the person who hurt you.

5. We then go to the Global Perspective as part of this thinking exercise. We all share a common humanity. The Global Perspective asks this of the forgiver: Is it true that every person on the planet has built-in or inherent worth that is unconditional, that does not have to be earned? Even from a biological perspective, the conclusion is that each person is unique and therefore special. That biological conclusion is reached when we realize that each of us has unique DNA. Thus, there never was another person on this earth just like you (with the possible exception of identical twins if DNA is the exclusive focus, which it should not be). Even in the case of identical twins, they retain their uniqueness through different experiences, different attitudes, different goals and choices in life, and most importantly in having distinct souls. So, too, are those who have hurt us unique and irreplaceable. With the Global Perspective, we are to see more deeply, more broadly, the inherent, built-in worth of all people, including those who are outside our door, dying on the streets, in your city or in Calcutta, and seeing the humanity in those who have hurt us. This can take time and effort. This takes training to become forgivingly fit.

6. We then move to the Cosmic Perspective, which is the transcendent perspective. Those in the Missionaries of Charity, for example, will embrace this perspective. Not everyone does. We never force someone to take this view toward the one who was unjust. The point here is to connect the other and you to

God. Listen to the wisdom of St. Teresa of Calcutta (2010): "Seeking the face of God in everything, everyone all the time" (*In the Heart of the World*). "The face of God in everyone"? Is this the case even for the ones who treat us unjustly? Yes. Both of you share being loved by God. This kind of insight can take time and this is why we do not start with the Cosmic Perspective, but instead with the other's woundedness through the Personal Perspective. Seeing wounds, even emotional wounds, is a more concrete exercise for some people than trying to see that the other is loved by God.

7. When we put together all three perspectives, we begin to see a genuine human being rather than evil incarnate. When we see this more complete person, who is more than the unjust behaviors, we notice that the forgiver's heart starts to soften toward this person. The rust of resentment begins to lessen. This can lead to the emergence of compassion or a willingness to suffer along with the one who was unjust. When the forgiver's heart softens in this way, this opens up the possibility of an internal unity within the forgiver, a unity with others because the forgiver is not displacing anger so much anymore onto others, and it even opens up the possibility of a unity with the offending person if he or she is open to a mutuality of respect or even love.

8. Only when the forgiver goes through the thinking exercises of the Personal, Global, and Cosmic Perspectives, only when compassion begins to emerge even in a small way do we move to the third point in the Work Phase, in which we ask the forgiver to bear the pain of what happened to him or her. To stand in the pain of what happened means that you do not throw that pain back to the one who hurt you. We have

a concrete image of bearing the pain. In fact, we have the perfect image of bearing the pain and it is Jesus Christ on His Cross. We are told to take up our Cross every day and to follow in His steps. As we take up our Cross for the one who hurt us, we are practicing Christian forgiveness.

If people do not bear the pain, and if that pain endures for years in the human heart, then that pain can be transferred to friends, to family members, to our own community. I consult with people in Northern Ireland regarding forgiveness education. When I walk through the malls of Belfast, I often see very angry eyes in some of the adolescents. I cannot help but think that this is inherited anger, transferred pain, from one generation to another. Did you know that Northern Ireland has a high suicide rate for young adult men compared with the rest of the United Kingdom? Is this the case because too many people have not yet stood up to their pain, passed it to their children, who passed it to their children, and on it has gone to the present generation? The pains of the past, even from hundreds of years ago, can be alive and existing in those who have inherited that pain. Forgiving is a way of breaking this cycle of inherited pain. And I certainly am not blaming parents here because this passing on of the pain almost always is unconscious, with the parents not even realizing this dynamic of one's own pain being transferred to the next generation. In other words, there absolutely is no intention on the parents' part to pass pain to their children.

9. Only after the forgiver has taken the three thinking perspectives, has begun to develop some compassion toward the one who offended, and has begun to bear the pain do we ask him or her to now truly exercise forgiveness as the moral virtue

that it is. We ask the person to consider giving a gift of some kind to the one who was hurtful. The point is to give something that is good directly to the person or indirectly to others, as in the kind word spoken about the person. This is not easy when one's heart is broken. From a worldly perspective, this is absurdity. After all, why be good to those who are not good to you? Yet, it is this giving that enlarges one's heart and makes the compassion all the stronger. That is the paradox of forgiving, to struggle, through your pain, to be kind, respectful, and even loving toward the one who was not kind, respectful, or loving to you. Did Jesus Christ offer these qualities to each of us from His Cross, even before we were born? Did He not offer these to us unconditionally so that we would come to Him, repent, and be reconciled to Him?

10. It then is in Phase Four, the Discovery Phase, that people begin to find meaning in the suffering and to find explicit purpose in one's life. We learn more deeply who Jesus Christ is, what our role is as forgivers, and that we have matured in our suffering. Do you know what many people's new purpose in life is once they have forgiven others for deep injustices? They now want to help others forgive, to unlock the shackles that have bound their heart, and to set free hurting people so that they can love more deeply. They want to become healers of others, not necessarily professionally, but they want to heal the woundedness in the world. It is here, near the end of the forgiveness process, that our science documents the paradox of forgiveness, a greater wholeness, more integrity, more healing in those who take the time to forgive.

11. A summary of this forgiveness process is below:

Table 1
Forgiveness Process Model for Healing

Preliminaries

✠ Who hurt you?

✠ How deeply were you hurt?

✠ On what specific incident will you focus?

✠ What were the circumstances at the time? Was it morning or afternoon? Cloudy or sunny? What was said? How did you respond?

PHASE ONE—UNCOVERING: Uncovering Your Anger

✠ How have you avoided dealing with anger?

✠ Have you faced your anger?

✠ Are you afraid to expose your shame or guilt?

✠ Has your anger affected your health?

✠ Have you been obsessed about the injury or the offender?

✠ Do you compare your situation with that of the offender?

✠ Has the injury caused a permanent change in your life?

✠ Has the injury changed your worldview?

PHASE TWO—DECISION: Deciding to Forgive

✠ Decide that what you have been doing hasn't worked.

✠ Be willing to begin the forgiveness process.

✠ Decide to forgive.

PHASE THREE—WORKING: Working on Forgiveness

✠ Work toward understanding (personal, global, and cosmic perspectives).

✠ Work toward compassion.

✠ Accept the pain.

✠ Give the offender a gift.

PHASE FOUR—DISCOVERY: Discovery and Release from Emotional Prison

✠ Discover the meaning of suffering.

✠ Discover your need for forgiveness.

✠ Discover that you are not alone.

✠ Discover the purpose of your life.

✠ Discover the freedom of forgiveness.

R. Enright (2019). *Forgiveness Is a Choice.* Washington, D.C.: APA Books; R. Enright (2012a). *The Forgiving Life.* Washington, D.C.: APA Books; R. Enright (2015). *8 Keys to Forgiveness.* New York: Norton.

JOURNAL REFLECTION: How would you describe the process of forgiving to someone who asked you about this road map which you just read?

CHAPTER 9

Scientific Evidence That Practicing Forgiving Is Good for the Forgiver

Examples of Experimental Studies (with Randomized Experimental and Control Groups) in Which People Forgive or Learn about Forgiveness

We have done many studies to aid people to forgive those who have been deeply unjust to them. We first screen the participants to be sure that they have a particular injustice. As you will see below, for example, the second entry concerns incest survivors and therefore only those who report such abuse would be further screened for possible participation in the study. Next, we screen for current psychological compromise such as excessive anger, depression, low self-esteem, and/or a low sense of hope for the future. We then randomly assign the participants to the experimental group, in which they go through the process of forgiveness described above, or to a control group. Sometimes in the control group, we simply have the participants wait until the experimental group completes the intervention and then those participants in the control group start the forgiveness intervention. In contrast, sometimes within the control group we provide an alternative activity, such as in the third entry below in which the participants engaged in the usual drug rehabilitation within that particular institution. The first eight entries below describe research with adult and adolescent samples and the final five entries describe forgiveness education with children and adolescents. In forgiveness education, we do not engage in direct forgiveness therapy, as in the adult samples. Instead, we introduce the child and adolescent participants to forgiveness through stories. They learn about forgiveness for the most part and only practice forgiving a classmate or a sibling if they choose to do so. As you will see, both forgiveness therapy and forgiveness education provide considerable improvement to a person's current well-being. This should not lead to a conclusion that the only or major point of forgiving is psychological health. We have such a focus because we approach the research from a mental health standpoint as researchers within a psychological context.

1. *Elderly women treated unjustly in the family context.* This is the study brought to your attention at the beginning of the Foreword. Following an 8-week forgiveness intervention with elderly females, those who had the forgiveness intervention showed significantly higher forgiveness at posttest compared with the control group. Both groups significantly decreased from pretest to posttest on psychological depression and trait anxiety (Hebl & Enright, 1993).

2. *Incest survivors.* The forgiveness group became emotionally healthier than the control group after fourteen months of the forgiveness intervention, which was one-on-one with the intervener for about one hour each week. Differences between the groups were observed for depression, anxiety, hope, and self-esteem. The results were maintained in a 14-month follow-up (Freedman & Enright, 1996). The control group started the forgiveness intervention once the first group completed it. They, too, had the 14-month intervention and they improved in a similar way.

3. *Drug rehabilitation.* The forgiveness participants met as a group twice a week for six weeks and became emotionally healthier than the control group, similar to the above study. The experimental participants' need for drugs declined substantially, relative to the control group. Results were maintained at a 4-month follow-up (Lin et al., 2004).

4. *Cardiac patients.* Again, the experimental (forgiveness) group became emotionally healthier than the control group after the 10-week intervention. At a 10-week follow-up, the experimental group had more efficiently functioning hearts than the control group (Waltman et al., 2009).

5. *Emotionally abused women.* In this study, women who were verbally abused by their husband, and who were divorced for at least two years, had a forgiveness intervention, one-on-one with the intervener for over thirty weeks for each participant. Results are similar to the above studies in terms of emotional health (decreased anxiety, depression, post-traumatic stress symptoms, increased self-esteem) (Reed & Enright, 2006).

6. *Terminally ill, elderly cancer patients.* After a four-week intervention, the forgiveness group showed greater improvement in psychological health (less anger, more hopefulness toward the future) than the control group. Physical indicators of both groups showed declines (Hansen et al., 2009).

7. *Abused early adolescent females in Pakistan.* One year after the forgiveness intervention, which was twice a week for four months, those in the forgiveness group had maintained their reduction in anger and their increase in hope for the future relative to the control group (Rahman et al., 2018).

8. *At-risk middle school students in Wisconsin.* After a fifteen-week in-school intervention, those in the experimental group not only improved more in emotional health than those in the control group but also they improved more in academic achievement than the control counterparts (Gambaro et al., 2008). *At-risk middle school and high school students in Seoul, Korea.* The findings are similar to the above study (Park et al., 2013).

9. *First Grade (Primary 3) children in Belfast, Northern Ireland.* After a seventeen-week intervention, those in the experimental group were less angry than those in the control group. Randomization is by group; analyses are on each individual (Enright et al., 2007).

10. *Third Grade (Primary 5) children in Belfast, Northern Ireland.* After a fifteen-week intervention, those in the experimental group were less angry and depressed and more forgiving than those in the control group (Enright et al., 2007).

11. *First Grade and Fifth Grade children in Milwaukee's central city.* Those in the experimental group (seventeen weeks for first grade and fifteen weeks of intervention for fifth grade) were less angry than those in the control group (Holter et al., 2008).

12. *Parents of Third Grade (Primary 5) children in Belfast, Northern Ireland* improved statistically (the parents improved), compared to the comparison group, in their forgiving people who hurt them as they taught forgiveness to their children in a fourteen-week intervention. The comparison group parents taught art to their children (Magnuson et al., 2009).

13. *Eighth Grade students in Iran.* Those in the experimental group were less angry and reduced more in prejudice relative to

those in the control group (Ghobary Bonab et al., 2021) after the fifteen-week intervention and the three-month follow-up.

JOURNAL REFLECTION: What insights do you have as you reflect on this area of research in the social sciences? How do you think people who read these studies in professional journals might respond to the idea of forgiveness?

CHAPTER 10

Filling Out the Personal
Forgiveness Scale

THE PURPOSE OF THIS chapter is to choose one person who has hurt your heart because of an act of injustice. This will be the person you will be forgiving as we advance in the book. After you finish the exercises in the book and have forgiven the person, it is my hope that you will start with another person and then yet another person. Why? Forgiving others is not a one-time act but a way of life as you continually grow in this vital moral virtue.

Try now to choose that one person who has wounded your heart because of an injustice toward you. You might have many people in mind, but I ask you to choose only one right now. It could be someone from your childhood, or your adolescence, or even someone who hurt you yesterday. This does not have to be the one person who has deeply crushed your heart, but at least someone who hurt you and you are not over it yet. In other words, as I stated above, you always can come back to this exercise with someone else, eventually with the one who has been the most unfair to you. You can forgive this person (who hurt you the most) after you have learned this pathway with other, less hurtful persons. Please take some time to choose the one whom you would like to start forgiving now.

This exercise concerns your *current level of forgiveness* toward the person. This is for your own private edification as to how you are doing on the forgiveness path. (Note: The Personal Forgiveness Scale below was first published in Enright, 2012a, and then featured in the magazine *Psychology Today*, January 2022).

Personal Forgiveness Scale

We are sometimes unfairly hurt by people, whether in family, friendship, school, work, or other situations. We ask you now to think of someone who has hurt you unfairly and deeply—someone who has wounded your heart. For a few moments, visualize in your mind the events of that interaction. Try to see the person and try to experience what happened.

Now, please answer a series of questions about your current attitude toward this person. We do not want your rating of past attitudes, but your ratings of attitudes right now.

Please rate each item on a 1-to-6 scale as follows:

1 = Strongly Disagree

2 = Disagree

3 = Slightly Disagree

4 = Slightly Agree

5 = Agree

6 = Strongly Agree

For each item, please rate the level of agreement that best describes your current feeling on the above scale. When indicated, place each word or phrase in the blank when answering each item.

This first set of items deals with your *current feelings or emotions right now toward the person.*

I. *I feel* _____ *toward him/her.*

    (1) warm _____

    (2) negative _____

    (3) kindness _____

    (4) dislike _____

    (5) happy _____

    (6) angry _____

This set of items deals with your *current behavior toward the person.*

II. *Regarding this person, I do or would* _____.

    (7) show friendship _____

    (8) avoid _____

    (9) aid him/her when in trouble _____

    (10) ignore _____

    (11) do a favor _____

    (12) not speak to him/her _____

This set of items deals with *how you currently think about the person.* Think about the kinds of thoughts that occupy your mind right now regarding this particular person.

III. I think he or she is _____.

    (13) of good quality _____

    (14) corrupt _____

    (15) a good person _____

IV. Regarding this person, I _____

    (16) disapprove of him/her _____

    (17) wish him/her well _____

    (18) condemn the person _____

Scoring

Now add up your scores as you recorded them for the following items: 1, 3, 5, 7, 9, 11, 13, 15, 17.

Important: Now *reverse score the remaining* items: 2, 4, 6, 8, 10, 12, 14, 16, 18. In other words, if you gave a rating of 1, score it as a 6; if you rated an item as a 2, give this a 5; if you rated an item as a 6, then give it a 1; and so on.

Add up your scores on all 18 items.

Interpretation of Your Total Score

If you scored between 18 and 40, you are low in forgiving this person at this point in time. This does not mean that you will not raise your score. If you so choose, you might consider engaging in the forgiveness process to rid yourself of resentment and possibly to improve your relationship (if you have had one with the person).

If you scored between 41 and 63, you are still somewhat low in forgiving, but obviously are getting closer to a psychological state that is not as angry and therefore perhaps not as vulnerable. The midpoint of the scale is 63 and so anything below this shows that you can improve your forgiveness response if you are motivated to enter the forgiveness process.

If you scored between 64 and 86, you are showing forgiveness, at least to a degree. You may have a minimally wounded heart, in need of some forgiveness, but not imperative if you wish to be emotionally free from the effects of others' injustices toward you.

If you scored between 87 and 108, then you are already forgiving or well on your way to even more forgiving toward that person. You probably do not need to go through the forgiveness process with this person.

> **JOURNAL REFLECTION:** Where are you with regard to your degree of forgiving the person whom you identified on this scale? Are you low in forgiving, in the middle, or high in forgiving? Are you ready to start the forgiveness journey with this person? If not, and if your score was below the median of 63, then what do you think you need to be willing to go on this journey of forgiveness?

Note: If your score was moderately high (above the median of 63) to high (in the 87 to 108 range) toward this person, I recommend that you choose a different person whom you still need to forgive. Fill out the scale with this new person in mind to see if, indeed, this is the case. The exercises to follow are based on the assumption that you still need to forgive the person.

CHAPTER 11

THE GUIDED PRIVATE REFLECTION: UNCOVERING PHASE

IT IS TIME FOR our first forgiveness journey. We will be using the Process Model of Forgiveness to start knowing more deeply what this pathway to forgiving is. This is the same pathway that we used in our scientific investigations which I described in Chapter 9. As we saw, those scientific studies showed statistical significance in people becoming healthier as they forgave people for deep injustices against them.

Because forgiveness is a moral virtue, this takes time to develop, to mature in you. Therefore, you likely will not complete this forgiveness journey (with the one you identified on the Personal Forgiveness Scale) as you read through this material one time only. Yet, as Aristotle reminds us, practice is important to grow in this heroic virtue of forgiving. So, your starting now, and revisiting this pathway in the future, will help you to deeply forgive the person.

This is not an exercise that you must push through or be in a hurry to accomplish. Take breaks from time to time. This journey is not like getting in a car and going directly from Point A to Point D in one hour. You will want to prayerfully reflect on some of the places we visit on this travel through forgiveness.

Also, please note that this exercise serves as a general introduction to this pathway of forgiving. We will not yet be engaging in the explicitly Catholic version of this pathway. That will come later.

We now will focus on the one person whom you identified on the Personal Forgiveness Scale. So, our first set of questions is to briefly recall the incident, not to replay it in detail in our minds, but to see it and know there was an injustice. Was it morning, afternoon, or evening? What was said? How do you remember responding? Please keep in mind that in this recalling of the incident, we now are moving toward healing from what happened.

Next, we enter the Uncovering Phase of the Process Model of Forgiveness. This phase asks you to examine the effects on you of the injustice. Sometimes we are surprised to learn that something which happened to us in the past is still having an effect on us years later. In this Uncovering Phase, I will be asking you 8 questions. Not all of them will apply to you. I ask all 8 for the sake of being as complete as I can. Each one of these can be a journal reflection for you.

1. The first question is this: Have you simply not considered the effects on you of what happened? Many people try to "just move on in life" and so they stop thinking about what happened, even though there still is anger or bitterness or sadness quietly sitting inside the heart. Has this happened to you? Have you not looked within to see if there still are very real effects of this injustice that remain unhealed for you? If so, please be gentle with yourself. This denial of negative effects within is common.

2. I now ask you to look within and ask a courageous question: Are you angry with this person for what happened? Are you more angry than you realized? It may not be anger. Instead, you might be sad or frustrated. Maybe it is a feeling of shock (How could this person do such a thing to me?). On the other hand, anger, as a description, might not go far enough. Maybe you are extremely angry or enraged. Do you have some kind

of a feeling inside of you right now that is an effect from what happened? If so, try to put a number on that feeling, with a 1 being very, very mild and a 10 being exceptionally intense. Where are you in your inner world on this on the 1-to-10 scale? A lot of times we have more of this emotion than we realize. The first step is to heroically realize that you have been hurt and you are carrying this now.

3. The third effect of what happened is shame and even feelings of guilt. Shame occurs when we do not want the light to shine on us; we want to hide under the bed. For example, some people might have whispered, "What did she do that brought all of this on?" Even though you are innocent, people can be judgmental and can talk. This can lead to shame. Do you have shame within you because of what happened?

Besides shame, we sometimes harbor a sense of guilt because of how we reacted to the other person. Maybe you said something that you regret. Guilt, as you know, is that inner conviction that you have broken a moral standard. Do you have guilt for how you responded then, or maybe how you talked with others about this person?

Unless you were responsible for the action, you do not deserve the shame or guilt which you now experience. Had the other not been unfair, you never would be experiencing either one of these. Yet, if you are experiencing shame or a feeling of guilt, these are secondary wounds from that original injustice. I only ask you here to see if shame or guilt feelings are living within you, rather than your trying at this point to reduce these.

4. Has the anger, sadness, frustration, or shame affected your health? Has what happened to you affected your well-being?

Do you know what is the most frequent issue that people see here? It is fatigue, being too tired for too long. You see, if you are carrying around all day and all night a big sack of resentment on your back, this can and will tire you. Are you tired from this injustice? If so, please do not be hard on yourself. You did not deserve this and this can be healed.

5. As the fifth effect, we see that a person can obsess over what happened, thinking over and over about it. Recall the young man from Chapter 8 whose father used to beat him as a child and this led to nightly dreams of his father chasing him. Do you think over and over about what happened to you? Sometimes we are driving our car and we start to almost subconsciously think about what happened, not paying full attention to our driving. As another example, we are watching a film and we lose focus as the person or the incident comes into our mind. This is a person's way of trying to solve the problem, but without forgiveness when the injustice was strong and your wounds deep, it is hard to heal. We need forgiveness to rid ourselves of the resentment that we did not deserve, that keeps popping up in our mind.

6. A sixth issue is this: Do you compare your situation with the one who hurt you? There was a Mr. Kiel (1986) who was a store owner. A person with a gun came into the store to commit a robbery. He shot and paralyzed Mr. Kiel. Over time, Mr. Kiel kept thinking about how this person who robbed is walking around on two healthy legs, never been found or arrested, while he (Mr. Kiel) will be in a wheelchair for the rest of his life. This thought intensified his rage and led to a clinical depression. Only upon forgiving the man whom he never met in any formal sense did the depression begin to ease for him. He was not able to reverse the effect of being paralyzed, but now

he does not struggle with paralysis and being depressed. He got rid of something very major in his life by forgiving the one who shot him. It was that constant comparison between the one who shot him and himself that was making it so difficult.

7. A seventh effect of being treated unjustly is this: Has the incident led to a major change in your life, perhaps a change you did not want to make? Consider from our Chapter 9 the women who were in the Reed and Enright (2006) study. They did not want the abuse and they did not want the divorce, if the husband were to change in a positive way. Some of them had to seek a new home or a new job. Some had to raise children alone. There were major life changes they had to face and so not only was there a divorce and social adjustments that had to be made, but also a growing toxic anger within most of them. Has this happened to you where you have had a significant change in your life that you did not want to make, that you did not deserve? Are you angry about it? Is it affecting you now?

8. An eighth effect is this: The injustice and all that you have experienced as effects (anger or sadness, shame, fatigue, rumination on what happened, unhelpful comparison between the other person and you, and/or a significant life-change) can affect your worldview, your philosophy of life, even the depth of your faith. What I tend to see is this: As people are hurt by others and remain unhealed, the worldview very slowly begins to change, to become more negative. As an analogy, think of a rowboat tethered to a dock. The rope slowly and imperceptibly loosens from that dock and the boat slowly begins to drift out to the middle of the lake. That rowboat is your worldview, which can become untethered from truth, goodness, and beauty as you slowly sink into a pessimism that, for example,

concludes: No person can be trusted; or, God has abandoned me. What used to be a positive, hopeful worldview has become more darkened because of the injustice and the subsequent pain within. Has this begun to happen to you? Are you more pessimistic today than in the past? Has your relationship with God become less trusting or more trusting over time? Some people blame God for what other people do from their own free will. Their worldview becomes distorted because of other people's distorted view of how they should treat others. If your worldview has changed to the more negative, this is not unusual. Again, please be gentle with yourself. The point of this and our subsequent forgiveness exercises is to reawaken a worldview that is based on truth, goodness, and beauty.

9. Summary of the Uncovering Phase as a Journal Reflection: Can you see how the poisons of injustice can be so very unfair? Not only has the injustice happened, but all of these other effects can come tumbling down on you and so you have within you all of these effects that can last a lifetime. What we have to do is challenge what is happening to us in these effects so that we can recapture what is true and good and beautiful. Some people "just move on," but where is the goodness in that? Where is the respect or generosity or love there? You can move on with a cold indifference. Moving on is not forgiveness. This ends the Uncovering Phase and it usually gets people's attention because, quite frankly, they are surprised to look within and see so many effects in need of healing. You don't deserve these effects of the injustice you suffered and you can get rid of them through forgiveness.

CHAPTER 12

THE GUIDED PRIVATE REFLECTION: DECISION PHASE

WE NOW ENTER OUR second of four phases, the Decision Phase. First, we have to decide that how we have been approaching this injustice has not worked. We then have to make a free-will decision of trying forgiveness. As we saw, the science does support forgiving as a viable way of healing from injustice's effects.

Are you willing to try forgiveness toward the person whom you identified on the Personal Forgiveness Scale? Again, the next three points can be part of your journal reflections.

1. How do you understand what forgiveness is? As a review: a) you have been treated unjustly; b) you willingly will work on getting rid of resentment toward this person; and c) you will strive at least eventually to be kind, respectful, generous, and even loving toward the one who hurt you. At the same time, you will not excuse the behavior. What happened to you was wrong, is wrong, and always will be wrong. You will not forget what is potentially harmful for you, so that you do your best to not have it happen again. You may or may not be able to reconcile with the other because he or she may not want to reconcile. When you forgive, you do not abandon the quest for justice. You can and should ask for fairness.

2. If you are willing to forgive, then I have a homework assignment for you. It includes only three words: Do no harm. Are you willing to commit now to do no harm to the one who hurt you? This might include not saying bad things about the person to others in your family or community. Certainly, you can talk with others about the person and what happened, but you will refrain from condemning that person. Can you see that this homework assignment is not asking you to start loving the other right now? Instead, it is asking you to refrain from the negative.

3. What if the person is deceased? How can one even harm the person now? While direct harm to the person's physical being will not happen, we still, for example, can destroy a person's reputation by what we say and how we say it. One can refrain from that and thus do no harm.

This homework assignment in Point 2 ends Phase 2 of the Decision Phase.

CHAPTER 13

The Guided Private
Reflection: Work Phase

We now enter the third of four phases, the Work Phase.

Work... effort... It is time for us to enter the forgiveness gym and become forgivingly fit. We will do some serious work on the moral virtue of forgiveness. This can take months, and so our going through this in a short period of time does not mean that our quest for forgiveness fitness now has ended. As getting into good physical shape takes time, so, too, it may be with forgiveness toward one particular person.

In my book *The Forgiving Life*, I talk about the free will (I choose to forgive), a good will (I know that forgiving is virtuous and I want to give this goodness), and a strong will (I will persevere over a long period of time). The Work Phase requires all three. It includes the strong will or not giving up and not becoming diverted by other demands of life and letting forgiveness fade within you.

So, as we open the gym door, we see four fitness stations. Let us take each one in order. Points two through eight are meant to be journal reflections for you.

1. The first exercise in the Work Phase is what we call the thinking exercises. It is easier to think about the one who hurt us than it is to feel warm feelings (at least at first) toward him or her. We are not always in control of our feelings. If I say, "Feel

warmly about someone who hurt you," that can be difficult. Yet, if I say, "Think of a purple elephant sitting on an orange tree," this you can do. Thus, it is easier to think about the other than to feel good feelings for him or her, at least right now.

There are three different thinking exercises for us: the Personal, Global, and what we call the Cosmic Perspectives. The Personal Perspective delves into the subjective, personal heart of the one who hurt you. As I pointed out in Chapter 8, if someone is robbed by a masked marauder on the Piazza Navona, the forgiver will not know the inner world of that person. Yet, I find that in most cases, those who hurt us tend to be the ones close to us, those in our family or community. Thus, most people can engage in this Personal Perspective.

2.   Here is my First Question: Is it possible that the one who hurt you was hurt by others prior to hurting you?

What was this person's life like while growing up? Did someone dump the truck of resentment onto this person a long time ago?

Might the person who hurt you have done so out of a wounded heart, a confused heart, a heart that has been damaged, and that person then damaged you? Is it possible that the one who hurt you is a wounded person from others in the past so that the wounds keep getting transferred to others in the future, like a virus jumping from one person to another?

Think about the person's heart and who damaged the person's heart. I am not excusing what the person did to you. The person still should not have hurt you, but I want you to see that, in all likelihood, this is more than someone who hovers over you with great meanness and this is all there is to him or her.

Is there doubt, confusion, shame, guilt, rumination, woundedness existing in the heart of this person? Has the person been crushed and now you have inherited that? I wish it had not happened to you and I wonder if a wounded person wounded you. This takes awhile to figure out, but I would like you to think about this.

3. Let us now turn to the Global Perspective. The Global Perspective asks about your shared humanity. One area of humanity that you likely share is this: You both share having been wounded. As we saw earlier, another is that you both share unique DNA. Both of you, thus, are special, unique, and irreplaceable. Once each of you passes away, there never will be another person quite like either of you on this planet ever again. What else do you share in common? When you are cut, you bleed. You both need adequate nutrition and rest to be healthy. Both of you will die one day. You share fallibility and you share mortality. You share much in your humanity.

Because both of you are unique in the world, it follows that both of you are special. Both of you are irreplaceable. Do you know what that means? It means that both of you have built-in or inherent worth that cannot be taken away from you, even when either of you behaves badly. You do not have to earn your worth. The one who hurt you does not have to earn his or her worth. For both of you, it is not only your behavior that determines your worth because that worth is built into you, not because of what you or the other do, but in spite of that.

Think about this for yourself. Just because you are a wounded person, this does not define who you are. If you have been defining yourself by your wounds, rise up beyond that, think more deeply about yourself. Yes, you carry wounds, but *you are carrying them,* heroically and courageously. Look at all you have done while carrying those wounds. You possess built-in worth. So does the one who has hurt you. Therefore, both of you share inherent worth. This insight takes time, so please be gentle with yourself.

4. Let us now move to the Cosmic Perspective. As stated earlier, we do not always use this way of thinking in our forgiveness road map because this is the transcendent perspective, going beyond the material world. This is the spiritual, the religious perspective and not everybody has that.

   For us, let us start with a new homework assignment. Let us read the first chapter of the Old Testament, Genesis 1. Notice this: We are all made in the image and likeness of God. Notice, importantly, that this is repeated in this same chapter. When words are repeated in the Bible, it is for the purpose of emphasis. In this very first chapter of this very first book, this important theme is repeated: We are all made in the image and likeness of God.

   Are you made in the image and likeness of God? If so, are you made to love?

   Now for an important question which may have a difficult answer for you: Is the one who hurt you made in the image and likeness of God? This may take time to sink into your thoughts and so, again, please be gentle with yourself.

   Recall now the "Our Loving Heavenly Father" exercise in Chapter 2. As a refresher, consider just three of those Bible quotations:

   > *John 3:16: For God so loved the world that he gave his only Son, that whoever believes in him should not perish but have eternal life.*

John 15:13: Greater love has no man than this, that a man lay down his life for his friends.

Romans 5:8: But God shows his love for us in that while we were yet sinners Christ died for us.

If God is love, does He love both the other and you unconditionally? I am not making the suggestion of a universal salvation here. As you well know, people have to be willing to feel sorry for their sins, repent, and follow in Jesus' steps. Yet, even without a universal salvation, God loves all and desires that no one should perish as we read in 2 Peter 3:9: "The Lord is not slow about his promise as some count slowness, but is forbearing toward you, not wishing that any should perish, but that all should reach repentance."

Please take a moment, then, to reflect on this: God loves me unconditionally. God loves unconditionally the one who hurt me.

5. Let us now put all of these perspectives together.

Who is the one who hurt you? He or she possibly is a wounded, confused, crushed person, who shares inherent worth with you in that both of you are special, unique, and irreplaceable, and you are both made in the image and likeness of God, loved unconditionally by Our Heavenly Father. Do you see right here and right now how that person is more than the unjust behaviors against you? Do you see how you are more than unjust behaviors against you? Those behaviors do not define that person any more than they define who you are. You are much more than that. The one who hurt you is much more than that. See the bigger picture of both of you so you can meet an "I" *with* an "I" rather than taking an "eye" *for* an "eye." See each of you as person-to-person, each in your own uniqueness, each sharing inherent worth because you both are made in the image and likeness of God.

Who is the one who hurt you?

Who are you as a person?

6. Now to our Second Question in the Work Phase. Once the thinking exercises are completed, we now ask this: As you begin seeing the other person in his or her woundedness, seeing that you share inherent worth, and seeing that both of you are made in the image and likeness of God, what is your heart like?

Center now on your heart as I again review the three kinds of perspectives toward the one who hurt you. Look for even a little compassion growing in you for this person. Compassion is a willingness to suffer along with the other in the other's suffering. It is a softening of the heart so that it is not stoney cold toward the other person. We are chiseling away at the hardness of the heart by letting in, for now, a little bit of warmth into your heart.

So, please listen again: 1) You both have been wounded and that does not define the other or you. 2) You both have inherent worth. Focus on the heart as you read this. 3) You both are made in the image and likeness of God. Does this make your heart a little softer toward the other person? If so, that is the beginning of bringing your more positive emotions into the moral virtue of forgiveness.

7. We now have a very important point, our Third Question in the Work Phase: Can you bear the pain of what happened to you so that you do not throw that pain back to the one who wounded you or to any other person?

When you see the person across the Personal, Global, and Cosmic Perspectives, when you see your heart getting a little less stoney cold, a little warmer, are you willing to stand in that pain and say, "It happened to me, I have pain, and I am not going to pass that pain back to the one who hurt me or to anyone else"?

Hospice workers, when counseling those who are grieving the passing of a loved one, suggest that they "lean into" the grief (emotions) and the mourning (behaviors such as crying) (Kron, 2020). The Israeli psychiatrist Morton Kaufman (1984) counseled his clients to bear the pain so that they do not displace that pain onto unsuspecting others.

Our quintessential example is Jesus Christ bearing our sins on His Cross out of love for us. We read in Isaiah 53:5: "But he was wounded for our transgressions, he was bruised for our iniquities; upon him was the chastisement that made us whole, and with his stripes we are healed."

Yet, with regard to bearing the pain for the other person, you might ask, "Won't this make me live with the pain for the rest of my life?" Actually, no, because forgiveness is a paradox. As you give to the one who hurt you, you receive the gift of emotional healing. As you accept the pain, and for the good of others, your pain begins to leave. It is when you hold the resentment that such a toxic emotion can stay with you for the rest of your life. As you let resentment fester and as you foster it, that is when the pain stays. Yet, as you say, "I will bear this pain for — for — the other and others," it is there that the pain begins to leave.

How do we know this? We have scientifically examined the outcomes of such forgiveness, as we saw previously. It is in the forgiving that anger, anxiety, and depression reduce statistically significantly. It is in the forgiving that hope for the future increases and people begin to like themselves again.

8. Let us now move to the Fourth Question in the Work Phase: Are you ready to give a gift to the one who hurt you? It is here that I hear howls of protest: But the person hurt me; I owe that person nothing. Why should I do all of the giving as he or she does all of the getting? This is unfair!

Yes, forgiveness is not about fairness because this moral virtue does not center on the moral virtue of justice. Instead, forgiveness comes out of *agape* love, or love in service to others in such a way that it can be painful for the forgiver. From *agape* comes mercy or giving people more than they deserve. Then comes the moral virtue of forgiveness in which we are kind, respectful, generous, and *agape* loving toward those who have been unfair to us. Forgiveness is about mercy, not getting what we deserve or what is fair to receive from the one who hurt us.

This is what makes forgiveness so very controversial in secular society because such societies run on justice, on laws. Forgiveness is so rarely discussed and so it is rarely understood. Thus, people consider it to be weak and even morally wrong. In other words, they are choosing in an "either-or" way, justice or forgiveness. They are not thinking more expansively in a "both-and" way, justice and forgiveness growing up together.

So, when we forgive, we consciously (free will) decide to be good to the one who hurt us (good will). Why? It is because this is what forgiveness is about in a deep sense. Yet, we should not expect to reach this deep sense of forgiveness right away. We wait until the mind has a wider view of the one who was unfair. We wait until the heart softens and you say yes to bearing the pain of what happened.

Only when you are ready, please think about giving a gift that is appropriate and tempered (not too small or too extravagant) in your particular situation. Maybe it is a returned phone call. Maybe it is a letter written and then mailed to the person. Maybe it is a kind word about this person to others or giving a little money to charity in the person's name. Maybe it is a prayer for the salvation of that person's soul. Can you see how you can even give a gift to the one who is deceased with this kind word (about the person to others) or a charitable donation or prayer? As you contemplate what kind of gift to give and when to give it, I recommend that you pray about this and be guided by the Holy Spirit in your decision.

CHAPTER 14

THE GUIDED PRIVATE REFLECTION: DISCOVERY PHASE

WE ARE NOW READY to discuss the Fourth Phase of the forgiveness process, the Discovery Phase.

I have five questions for your journal reflection in this phase and two follow-up questions.

1. For our First Question, have you found meaning in your suffering? Viktor Frankl (1946), who was a survivor of the Auschwitz concentration camp during World War II, said that he found two kinds of people there, those who found meaning in their suffering and they lived and those who found no meaning in their suffering and they died. Finding meaning, in other words, is very important. What sense do you make of the suffering which you have endured? In my own experience in talking with others, many people tell me that once they forgive, a primary meaning in their suffering is that they become much more sensitive to other people's suffering. They see more clearly the inner wounds of all with whom they interact. They become aware that the inner world of other people may be more fragile than appears on the surface. Forgiveness gives people the eyes to see.

2. As our Second Question in the Discovery Phase, do you see that forgiving and being forgiven fit together? People who walk the path of forgiving now realize that some of their own sins have wounded others and so they are more motivated to go to those others and ask for forgiveness. We will discuss this idea of seeking forgiveness in more depth in Book Two, Chapters 11–13.

3. As a Third Question here, do you realize that you are not alone in your forgiving? You have the help of grace, as you ask Our Heavenly Father for help in your forgiving, which will bring that forgiving to a deeper and more complete level. We talk with others about our forgiveness journey, we read books. We are not alone as we walk this path.

4. As our Fourth Question, have you found a new purpose in life as you deliberately walk the path of forgiving with your free will, good will, and strong will? I find that many who are cleansed of resentment through forgiving have the new purpose in life of alleviating the suffering of others. This does not mean that they become mental health professionals. Instead, this becomes a life's goal. I once spoke with a gentleman who likely was going to spend the rest of his life in a correctional institution. He said this to me: Even though I will not be released from behind bars, I now have as a mission the helping of others to forgive.

5. Finally, we have our Fifth Question for you: Do you sense that you are being released from the emotional prison of resentment? Is your heart lighter and are you happier? This is where our science has centered, on the positive effects of countering the negative effects of the injustice which you have endured.

6. Now please recall my earlier question: On a 1-to-10 scale, how serious is your anger or sadness or depression or frustration? Do you recall what that number was then? What is that number now? Has it gone down to some degree? That is the beginning of inner healing if it has gone down even a little. Even if that number has not gone down, then we start the forgiveness process again with our strong will. We start with the Uncovering Phase and continue through the phases again and then once again ask ourselves the question of where we are on this 1-to-10 scale. Eventually that pain shrinks and it can leave. This is a fallen world. We may not be cleansed of all anger, but the big difference is this: The anger might have been controlling you; now you are in control of the anger, the sadness, whichever emotion has been part of you.

7. What does forgiveness do? It gets rid of the effects of unjust treatment against you. It is a sweeping out of the poison that we may not have even realized came to visit us and then settled in to stay. Forgiveness asks the poison to leave and it does.

Redemptive Suffering with Christ for the Other

CHAPTER 1

Forgiveness as Redemptive Suffering

In Book Two, I want to go as deeply as I am able to go in our understanding and application of forgiving. This does not mean that we are reaching the pinnacle of our understanding the idea of forgiving others. What it does mean is this: We will be going as far as I am able to see as I write this, which surely is imperfect. As Aristotle reminds us, none of us has a perfection in any of the moral virtues. In this discussion of what I see as the deepest views regarding forgiveness, I see that this depth is centered in Catholic thinking. Yes, it is my humble opinion that the Catholic views of forgiving are the deepest, the richest, the most important and accurate that I have ever seen.

Surely, the study of forgiving from philosophy and psychology can bring about healing for people and our science shows that to be the case, but the absolute depth of forgiving, to me, is found within the Catholic Church. It is found in the theology of redemptive suffering. In other words, to forgive is to redemptively suffer for the one who hurt us. We first will discuss what redemptive suffering is. After that, we will engage in the Private Guided Reflection again, but this time from the explicit Catholic perspective.

Let us examine the theme of redemptive suffering now with seven points. Here is what I have come to learn about redemptive suffering from the Catholic Church.

1. God is a community of Persons: Father, Son, and Holy Spirit. You are in community one with another because God is a community of persons. Community is important to keep in mind regarding forgiveness.

2. We are all made in the image and likeness of God (Genesis 1:26–27). Therefore, we are made for community with each other and with God. This is our nature, to be in community. We are made deliberately to be in community.

3. The central feature of our communion with each other is love because God is love (1 John 4:8), as we saw in our first exercise in Chapter 2 of Book 1.

4. If we are in communion with Jesus, and if His deepest communion with us is His love in the form of suffering, death, and resurrection, then we are to be in communion with Jesus in His suffering, death, and resurrection. If Jesus' concrete, specific form of love is suffering, death, and resurrection, then our form of love needs to be similar. In other words, our deepest experience of love is when we, with our free will, good will, and strong will, enter into Christ's particular way of love with Him, when we not only *imitate* Him (Ephesians 5:1–2; 1 Thessalonians 1:6–7) but also *unite* with Him (John 17:20–21). This is a very important distinction, between imitating Jesus and uniting with Him. Uniting is more important than imitating. Imitating occurs when we see another and copy the person's ways. When we unite we are engaged in a togetherness; we are coming together. Reflect on unity in John 17:20–21: "I do not pray for these only, but also for those who believe in me through their word, that they may all be one; even as thou, Father, art in me, and I in thee, that they also may be in us, so that the world may believe that thou hast sent me." It is our

unity with Jesus that shows the apathetic world that we are on to something wonderful and eternal.

JOURNAL REFLECTION: What is the difference between imitating Christ and being in union with Him?

5. Let us make a distinction between taking up one's Cross (Matthew 16:24) *for Christ* compared with *being crucified with Christ* (Galatians 2:20; 6:17). If we are to be with Jesus in love with Him, we are not only to take up our Cross, but also we are to be crucified with Christ, and this is biblical. In our first five points, we have gone from imitating to uniting with Christ, from taking up our own Cross to unity with Christ on His Cross with Him. This is a whole different dimension from imitating by taking up our Cross over there and being united in love with Jesus on His Cross with Him. This kind of unity takes work and takes the grace of God.

JOURNAL REFLECTION: What is the difference between taking up our cross for Christ and being crucified with Him?

6. If His love is for us and for others, then our love is to be for Him and for others, in the form of Jesus' suffering love for others (John 13:34–35; 15:12–14; Galatians 2:20; 6:17). This is how we are to live the forgiving life, in the form of suffering love. Let us reflect on John 15:12–14: "This is my commandment, that you love one another as I have loved you. Greater love has no man than this, that a man lay down his life for his friends. You are my friends if you do what I command you." How are we to love? " ... as I have loved you." Here we see the communion with Jesus. And how has Jesus loved us? He has done so out of

His crucified love, by laying down His life for His friends. So am I, are you, to lay down our life for others? That is the way it looks from the biblical perspective. We have to develop into that, and I think forgiving is one of the pathways into holiness. We can forgive for many reasons such as self-healing, healing of the other, and healing of the relationship. Yet, there is more. When we forgive, we are to be in unity with Jesus for the one who harmed us. There is a depth to forgiving that the world is missing. There are hundreds of scientific journal articles on forgiveness and they all miss this point.

7. As I asked in my presentation at the Theology Symposium in Maynooth, Ireland, in June 2012, why cannot we join Him from a safer distance? We see in 1 Peter 4:13 that we are to share in His suffering (*pathema*), not just admire or imitate Him: "But rejoice in so far as you share Christ's sufferings, that you may also rejoice and be glad when his glory is revealed." Imitation and union are not the same thing. First Jesus tells us in John to love as He does and then Peter tells us to share Jesus' suffering and then St. Paul in Colossians 1:24 tells us to rejoice in our suffering as we join with Jesus. Three writers and three common themes: Love as Jesus loved and do so with Him on the Cross to complete the nature of *agape* love.

JOURNAL REFLECTION: What is your response when you hear that we are to suffer *with* Christ? What does this mean for you as a person?

forgiveness is suffering

CHAPTER 2

REDEMPTIVE SUFFERING FROM POPE SAINT JOHN PAUL II

LET US TAKE A look at redemptive suffering as it refers specifically to our suffering with Christ for others. Redemptive suffering has its most complete discussion in Pope Saint John Paul II's *Salvifici Doloris* (1984). I find it interesting that this was published about a year after the assassination attempt on his life. It happened after he suffered gravely. Then came *Salvifici Doloris*. His suffering probably led to his giving us wisdom on suffering. In this soaringly excellent apostolic letter, Pope Saint John Paul II gives us vital insights into redemptive suffering that have direct relevance for us as we forgive others. Let us examine these now.

1. St. Paul, in Colossians 1:24, states: "In my flesh I complete what is lacking in Christ's afflictions for the sake of his body, that is, the church." What possibly could be lacking in the perfect Cross work of Christ? It is a perfect act of mercy and of justice. Actually, nothing is lacking in His perfect action of love. Instead, what is missing is the completion of that love, the completion of his suffering love by our love. As Pope St. John Paul II (in Section 24, third paragraph) clarifies: "the Redemption, accomplished through satisfactory love, *remains always open to all love* expressed in *human suffering*. In this

dimension — the dimension of love — the Redemption which already has been completely accomplished is, in a certain sense, constantly being accomplished." Love, to be completed, requires the participation of the other. Consider Pope Benedict's (Ratzinger, 2007, pg. 262) idea on this: "The fruit the Lord expects of us is love — a love that accepts with him the mystery of the Cross, and becomes a participation in his self-giving." What is lacking in the Cross work of Jesus Christ? It is your yes to participating in that love, your loving Jesus as He calls to you in love. You then are united to Him in suffering love. And where does this suffering love bear fruit? It bears fruit on the Cross with Christ ("accepts with him the mystery of the Cross," as we just saw in Ratzinger, 2007).

Notice that St. Paul is doing this for the Church. The Church is under siege right now with people thinking that the Catholic way is a usurper of freedom.

As a technical point here, the word *afflictions* in Colossians 1:24 in Koine Greek is *thlipsis*, meaning anguish, persecution, or tribulation. This, as we saw, is the anguish of love unfulfilled (lacking) until we join in love with Him. Does this mean that we share only Jesus' love and not His Passion? No, it seems that we share love with Him *in* His Passion based on what we just saw in 1 Peter 4:13 in Chapter 1 in this Book Two. To "share Christ's suffering" includes, as mentioned above, the Greek word *pathema*, a derivative of the word *pathos*, or passion, used consistently in the context of Jesus' actual Passion. See, for example, Luke 9:22, where Jesus Himself tells us of His upcoming suffering, death, and resurrection and uses the word *pascho* or *patho*. St. Paul did not use the word *pathos* in Colossians 1:24 (when referring to his completing Christ's *afflictions*) because nothing is lacking in the Passion.

> **JOURNAL REFLECTION:** Might your redemptive suffering, done with Jesus and for the Church, strengthen the barque of Peter as it takes on water in the stormy seas of secularism?

2. This is a "final discovery," not one easily recognized at the beginning of one's walk with Christ. We develop into this insight and so it takes time to mature. Because of this, the insight of redemptive suffering is missing for many, many people. We can accelerate this discovery by bringing this to others. You can help people discover love that they might have missed. There is nowhere else but the Catholic Church where people can get this information.

3. St. Paul's sufferings are accompanied by joy. Suffering finally has meaning. "Now I rejoice in my sufferings for your sake" (Colossians 1:24). The paradox of our suffering is that it can be the path to joy. As you can see from the first point above, by your saying yes to Jesus' love, you can enter into a deep, fulfilling love with your Savior. Wasn't it the same for Jesus? His suffering led to the resurrection, to joy eternal. This joy is another paradox. Recall we talked earlier about forgiveness as a paradox, giving goodness to those who were not good to you. As we enter into suffering love with Jesus in His afflictions to complete His love (Colossians 1:24) and as we enter into that suffering love specifically in His Passion (in other words, on His Cross with Him, 1 Peter 4:13), we eventually will find joy. When we suffer, we are not suffering alone. We are suffering with Jesus and doing so on His Cross, suffering love to suffering love.

> **JOURNAL REFLECTION:** How might this lead to joy for you?

4. Pope St. John Paul II further clarifies: "Human suffering has reached its culmination in the Passion of Christ. And at the same time it [our suffering] has entered into a completely new dimension and a new order: *it has been linked to love*" (*Salvifici Doloris*, no. 18). This insight completely changes the meaning of suffering. Suffering is not only about enduring but about growing, particularly using this opportunity to grow more deeply in your love "with Jesus, for Jesus, and to Jesus" (Mother Teresa, 1985, pg. 97). Suffering no longer is this grim situation to avoid at all cost. This is because our suffering now is linked to love.

JOURNAL REFLECTION: How might this unity with Christ have practical implications for how you live your everyday life?

5. "Christ has in a sense opened his own redemptive suffering to all human suffering. In so far as man becomes a sharer in Christ's sufferings — in any part of the world and at any time in history — to that extent *he in his own way completes* the suffering through which Christ accomplished the Redemption of the world" (Section 24, second paragraph). You are playing a part in the redemptive suffering of the world by uniting your suffering love with Jesus' suffering love on the Cross. Your love may be playing a part in the eternal salvation for those whom you serve and those for whom you pray. Your suffering is not for nothing.

JOURNAL REFLECTION: How might your suffering be given to you in part as a way to help save a soul or souls?

6. Does this mean that Christ's sacrifice was and remains incomplete? Did Jesus need us to complete suffering? As we already have seen in Section 24 of *Salvifici Doloris*: "No. It only means that the Redemption, accomplished through satisfactory love, *remains always open to all love*, expressed in *human suffering*" (Section 24, third paragraph). He is allowing us in. As an analogy, suppose you are building a sand castle on the beach. A cute three-year-old asks, "Can I help you build the sand castle?" You do not need the three-year-old to help you. Yet, out of love, you are leaving something open for the three-year-old. Jesus does the same with us and our love with Him on His Cross. He does not need us there, but He welcomes us out of love. We, in our fallen nature, do not necessarily understand completely how our part in Jesus Christ's redemptive suffering works. It is similar with the three-year-old, who does not understand the full dimensions of cooperation, love, and how the sand castle is completed. Yet, the loving cooperation does lead to the endpoint of the castle being constructed. Jesus Christ's redemptive work, as He invites us into the process, is accomplished according to His absolute will regardless of our insights, or lack of these, into this salvific work.

JOURNAL REFLECTION: What insights do you have as you reflect on the sand castle image?

7. The descriptions of redemptive suffering in *Salvifici Doloris* are consistent with the teachings within the *Catechism of the Catholic Church*. Consider two statements within the *Catechism*: paragraph 1505: "By his passion and death on the cross Christ has given a new meaning to suffering: it can henceforth configure us to him and unite us with his redemptive Passion."

Paragraph 1521: "Suffering, a consequence of original sin, acquires a new meaning; it becomes a participation in the saving work of Jesus."

8. Here we now focus on forgiveness and redemptive suffering. As a person suffers because of another's injustice, the one who suffers in forgiving has the opportunity to enter into redemptive suffering, with Jesus Christ, for that other person. This is what you can be doing when you forgive. You are in pain. You now can unite with Jesus in your pain for this other person who hurt you, who crucified you. The forgiver plays a part in the unjust person's salvation. This changes the meaning of what forgiving is. Your forgiving others who hurt you now is linked to love, and more precisely "with Jesus, for Jesus, and to Jesus" (Mother Teresa, 1985, pg. 97). We are not just trying to be kind to those who were unkind to us. As we in our suffering ask Jesus to save this person, this is sacrificial love. Forgiving now is linked to one's own suffering, the suffering of the unjust person or persons who offended, Jesus Christ's suffering, His suffering love and resurrection, and to experiencing a glimpse of one's own resurrection and aiding in the unjust one's actual resurrection to eternal life.

JOURNAL REFLECTION: What does forgiveness now mean to you?

9. The forgiver suffers for the other and his or her salvation; the forgiver is a gift of self to the other. This becomes a very personal action of an "I" suffering for another "I," the one who hurt you. This very personal giving of the self is explained this way by Pope Saint John Paul II (Section 29, first paragraph):

"We could say that suffering, which is present under so many different forms in our human world, is also present in order to unleash love in the human person, that unselfish gift of one's 'I' on behalf of other people, especially those who suffer." We talked earlier about giving a gift to the other. Here, even the idea of "gift" changes. Do you know what (whom) the gift is? That gift is you. Your very personhood is THE gift, which is different from giving A gift. This even changes the meaning of who you are. You are GIFT. I will not even put the word "a" before the word "gift."

> **JOURNAL REFLECTION:** Please reflect on this reality: You are gift.

10. Following Jesus' giving us the Lord's Prayer in Matthew (6:14–15), He gives commentary only on the theme of forgiveness in that prayer, and nothing else. Can we now see why Jesus' exclusive commentary on the Lord's Prayer was focused on forgiving? It is because forgiving is tied to our own and others' salvation.

> **JOURNAL REFLECTION:** Please reflect on why forgiveness is Jesus' exclusive commentary on the Lord's Prayer.

11. "It is precisely *the Church*, which ceaselessly draws on the infinite resources of the Redemption, introducing it into the life of humanity, *which is the dimension* in which the redemptive suffering of Christ can be constantly completed by the suffering of man" (Section 24, last paragraph). The insights you are receiving from *Salvifici Doloris* have emerged precisely through the Catholic Church.

> **JOURNAL REFLECTION:** What does this mean to you person-
> ally? It is in the Church where this is proclaimed, understood,
> developed, and acted upon.

12. As a side note, some of our separated brethren take offense at
this idea of people playing a part in the redemption because,
after all, Jesus' redemption was perfect and therefore sufficient. Catholics agree. As we focus on love we see that Christ
left something open for us, so that we can join Him in love for
others. We do not diminish Christ by these actions. Instead, we
fulfill love.

As a second issue for some of our separated brethren, they
argue that the Crosswork of Christ happened once and once
only and so people cannot now join Him on His Cross. Yet,
as Pope St. John Paul II (Section 24, paragraph 2) explains,
the Church, through the Mass and especially the Eucharist,
makes Jesus Christ's once-and-for-all sacrifice present to
us across historical time when he says: "The mystery of the
Church is expressed in this: that already in the act of Baptism,
which brings about a configuration with Christ, and then
through his Sacrifice — sacramentally through the Eucharist — the Church is continually being built up spiritually as
the Body of Christ. In this Body, Christ wishes to be united
with every individual, and in a special way he is united with
those who suffer." Pope Benedict XVI (2006, pg. 18) makes a
similar point: "We can thus understand how *agape* [sacrificial
love] also became a term for the Eucharist: there God's own
agape comes to us bodily, in order to continue his work in us
and through us."

It is sad that, as people leave Mother Church, they are leaving the forum, the fertile field in which all of this can take place.

So this message that we are contemplating here is going to be dying in the minds and hearts and souls of many, many people. Sadly again, this vital message is going to die fast and hard as the flood gates open and people leave the Church, their gateway to salvation and to profound forgiving in this world. You are the flame to keep this alive and if you do not, who will?

13. Jesus never will let His Church be abandoned. We know that, but this is a time of challenge. This is a time of redemptive suffering for us as people tell us that we are behind the times, as people tell us that we are prejudicial, and stereotypical, hateful, and bigoted. They will tell you that because they are not starting with the first premise, that God is Love. Yet, if we start with that premise that God is Love, we move to the insight that God is a community of Persons. If God is a community of Persons, and if I am made in the image and likeness of God, then I am made to be in community as well. I therefore am to be in community with Jesus. In what kind of community am I to participate with Jesus? It is the kind of community that completes what is lacking in His affections, which then changes the meaning of what suffering is, which changes the idea of what love is, which changes the idea of what forgiving is. As we saw in Point 9 above, it even changes what "gift" means.

14. Forgiving is getting to know Jesus on His Cross in unity with Him, suffering love to your suffering love, for the one who made you suffer. This likely will change the meaning of your relationship with Jesus. This relationship becomes a very personal, intimate form of love with Jesus, not some kind of generalized feeling of love for all people, most of whom you will never come to know. You enter into that "I" with an "I" relationship, as we discussed in Chapter 13 of Book One. In actuality here, the relationship is even more profound than "I" with an "I" because you now enter into an "I" with the "I AM" relationship, connecting deeply with the eternal God as you suffer, for now, for the one who hurt you and possibly sinned against God. You are suffering with the "I AM" Who is and was and is to come (Revelation 1:8). Forgiving, therefore, is more than extending your hand, which the other person broke, to help him or her out of the pit. Now you are going to be forgiving "with Jesus, for Jesus, and to Jesus" (Mother Teresa, 1985, pg. 97) with your love to help that person to salvation. This gives a new purpose to forgiveness. A strong will should aid you in persevering in this understanding, acceptance of this insight, and its direct application toward those who hurt you in this fallen world. Let this grow in your heart because the world needs this approach to forgiving now perhaps more desperately than ever.

JOURNAL REFLECTION: What now is forgiving for you?

Helping a person to
salvation.

CHAPTER 3

Clarifying What Redemptive Suffering Is prior to Our Forgiving Others through Such Suffering for Them

1. Before we begin an exercise of forgiving a person by redemptively suffering for him or her, let us take some time to further explore what redemptive suffering is in this context. I have seen the term *redemptive suffering* discussed in several different ways. Here are five examples that you might see if you begin reading in this area:

   As a person suffers, he or she turns toward God. People's own suffering, thus, helps them to be saved because they run to God as a way to get rid of the suffering. Notice that this is suffering for the self.

2. As a person sees the suffering that he or she caused to another, then the offender repents, turns toward God, and is saved. The offended person's suffering played an *indirect* part in helping the offender to repent. It is *indirect* because the offended person may have had no intention to play a role in saving the offending person.

3. As a person suffers, he or she may deliberately unite that suffering with Christ's suffering for the person's (the self's) own good. As in Point 1 above, this is redemptive suffering for the

self, not for others. It seems to be a higher level of redemptive suffering than Point 1 because here there is a deliberate, conscious attempt to unite with Christ in suffering (as opposed to running to Christ to take away the suffering).

4. As a person suffers an injustice from another person, the offended person may deliberately (with an intention to do so) unite that suffering with Christ's suffering for the good of the offending person (not for the good of the self). This is a more Christ-like suffering than 1, 2, or 3 because it is self-less. The uniting with Jesus includes *agape* love, the love that can be painful for the one who offers it to others.

5. As a person suffers, he or she may deliberately unite that suffering with Christ's suffering for the good of the offending person (not for the good of the self) as in 4 above, with the addition of expanding his or her love to include not just the person who offended but also many people. For example, a husband may redemptively suffer for his wife, who offended him, and then offer his suffering for the strengthening of all marriages in the world. Point 5 is a more expansive love than 4. Our challenge to you: Try to redemptively suffer in this selfless and lovingly expansive way. Why would we extend our redemptive suffering from one person to others as well? It is because we are a community of persons, made in the image and likeness of the Triune God, Who is a community of Persons. This to me is the highest level of redemptive suffering because we both keep redemptive suffering on the specific person-to-person level and take that suffering to the community level.

Journal reflection: What is redemptive suffering and is it important to you?

CHAPTER 4

QUESTIONS AND ANSWERS
AT THIS POINT IN OUR
EXPLORATIONS OF FORGIVING

THE FOLLOWING QUESTIONS HAVE been asked of me as I give talks on this subject of forgiveness, redemptive suffering, and the Catholic faith.

1. If the world is growing cold, should we expect more suffering?
    Yes, both within others and within ourselves. I talked recently with a Catholic priest from Ireland. He said, "People used to die for the faith here. Now they are leaving the faith." He was worried about their souls as well as their interactions with others that could become less gentle, less loving as he sees an anger in some of them.

2. Do you think it is similar now to what the early Church martyrs had to endure?
    As some become hostile toward the Christian faith now, I think there is a huge difference between what happened in the early Church and what is happening now. Following the wisdom of Hilaire Belloc, let us look at Christianity as a mountain, going up from the left, then to the pinnacle of truth, and then down to the right. The early Christians were going up the mountain, to the summit of truth. Today, with so many leaving the Church, they are going down the

mountain, away from the truth and the light. In Hilaire Belloc's words:

A man going uphill may be at the same level as another man going downhill; but they are facing different ways and have different destinies. Our world, passing out of the old Paganism of Greece and Rome towards the consummation of Christendom and a Catholic civilization from which we all derive, is the very negation of the same world leaving the light of its ancestral religion and sliding back into the dark. (Belloc, 1938)

Five years after Belloc's parable, Archbishop Fulton Sheen echoed a similar theme in the middle of World War II: "We are at the end of an era of history, just as definitely as Rome was at the end of an era when Alaric knocked at its Salarian gates. The difference between that crisis and ours is that in the case of Rome a material civilization was collapsing and a spiritual about to emerge. In the present instance, it is the spiritual which is being submerged and the material which is in the ascendancy" (Sheen, 1943).

Those going down the mountain have had a full revelation of the crucifixion and resurrection of Jesus Christ. Yet, they reject this revelation and therefore reject Christ. What they see, at the bottom of the mountain, is far different than what the early Christians saw as they looked up to the truth and the light. The suffering of those going down the mountain, away from Christianity, likely will be graver now.

2 Peter 2:20–22 strongly implies that this suffering is the case: "For if, after they have escaped the defilements of the world through the knowledge of our Lord and Savior Jesus

Christ, they are again entangled in them and overpowered, the last state has become worse for them than the first. For it would have been better for them never to have known the way of righteousness than after knowing it to turn back from the holy commandment delivered to them."

We will have to get ready for that in our own redemptive suffering. The early Christians were looking up toward the good, the true, and the beautiful while the new group is looking down with no true meaning to life. Where we are and what we are seeing from that vantage point makes a considerable difference.

3. The image of the three-year-old and the sandcastle is interesting. Jesus does not insist on her helping, does He?

Right! Jesus is such a gentleman that He does not insist. It is from our free will that we want to help build that sandcastle with Him. Of course, He is eager to love and to be loved, but the decision to come to Him is up to each of us.

4. The psychology of forgiveness seems less deep than the theology of forgiveness. Would you agree?

Yes. The idea of standing in the pain is qualitatively different between psychology and Catholic theology. In the theology, as we saw, the meaning of suffering differs radically because that suffering is linked to love. The essence of forgiveness also differs radically between the two disciplines. As with suffering, forgiveness is transformed in Catholic theology in that it becomes suffering love for the salvation of those who are unjust to us. Thus, both the meaning of suffering and forgiveness go much deeper in Catholic theology.

5. Can people get overwhelmed when they suffer if they do not know about redemptive suffering?

I do think so. As Pope Saint John Paul II instructs us, we need not grow bitter when we suffer. Instead, suffering is a stepping stone to growing in love both for Jesus and for persons. I see people who are going down that mountain become bitter and that bitterness transfers to God. Now they have the suffering and the willed severing of their relationship with our loving God. This would multiply the suffering, which then might multiply the bitterness. This is why we need to get this message to people. Therefore, we need this depth of theological understanding so we can bring it to others. Do you know where this starts? In each of our hearts. It starts with the interior life. You in community can help one another to develop this idea, this way of being with others. It starts with deepening our relationship with the crucified and resurrected Jesus Christ and then giving it to the world.

6. What if people are afraid to suffer?

Apprehension is normal, isn't it, when it comes to pain? Yet, with this way of thinking about and experiencing suffering, there is a way out. Suffering is not some isolated experience anymore because it is linked to love. It is that love, "with Jesus, for Jesus, and to Jesus" (Mother Teresa, 1985, pg. 97), that can lower the apprehension. Outside of the Catholic Church, I have never heard or read anything even close to this, that to forgive is to lovingly suffer with Jesus and then to love the one who injured us.

JOURNAL REFLECTION: With which of the answers above do you agree? With which of the answers above do you disagree and why? I do not agree w/ the Catholic Church

Guided Private Reflection with Redemptive Suffering as the Foundation: Uncovering Phase

TODAY, WE WILL CONTINUE to forgive the exact same person whom you started to forgive in Chapters 11 to 14 of Book One. This time, we will be approaching forgiving from the Catholic perspective. This one is the living, breathing Catholic experience. Please keep in mind that, as the ancient philosophers Plato and Aristotle remind us, and as St. Thomas Aquinas instructs, forgiving those who hurt us can take time (see, for example, Simon, 1986). In other words, this exercise in which we are about to engage is not a beginning and ending of your forgiving the person. You likely will have to revisit these exercises over weeks or even months because forgiving those who hurt us deeply can take time.

Let us quiet ourselves and think once again about the one person who has hurt us, the broken person, who might have broken our hearts. Let us recall the injustice. Let us call it what it is. Let us call it unfair and now that unfairness is in need of a response.

Let us start with a brief prayer: We now are going to walk our own Via Dolorosa, our own Way of the Cross, with You, Lord Jesus Christ, through the Uncovering Phase, the Decision Phase, the Work Phase, and the Discovery Phase of forgiveness. We ask You to be with us, Lord Jesus Christ, on this path so that we may grow closer to You, more intimately in love with You, and share our suffering with You. Amen.

Let us now enter the forgiveness process with the Uncovering Phase. We will take another look, with Jesus Christ, at the effects we still have. As before, each one of these can be a journal reflection for you.

1. First, are we in denial of the pain? For example, on the 1–10 scale, how much pain do you have in your heart right now? It is all right to admit it because you are doing this with Jesus Christ.

2. Another question I have for you is this: How would you label that pain? Is it anger? Is it disappointment? Sadness? Frustration? How would you label that? As you label it, is the number you assigned to this pain in number 1 above (on the 1–10 scale) more or less or about the same?

3. As you connect in love with Jesus, as you examine the extent of your pain from the effects of the injustice, were you shamed as Jesus was shamed on the Cross? If so, you now share that in common with Him. The Son of Man was tortured, spit upon, reviled, made a mockery with a crown of thorns. Notice how you share shame with Jesus. That certainly is nothing for which you should be ashamed as you share this with the crucified Christ.

4. What about your health? Let us think about that for a moment as an effect of the injustice. Have you been distracted? Have you been tired? Have you actually fallen beneath the weight of your Cross? As we know, Jesus fell three times. It is all right to fall. It seems to me that Jesus gives you permission to fall. He understands because He has done that, falling, for you. Just take a moment to reflect on your health and at times you may have truly stumbled beneath the weight. Jesus had Simon of Cyrene to help Him; you have Jesus Himself to come alongside you.

5. As another effect, have you internalized the injustice so that
   it lives within you, so that the person's actions are living ✓
   inside of you? This is another way in which you can stumble
   and fall.   don't allow a bitter root

6. As yet another effect, do you compare yourself with the one
   who hurt you? In other words, do you see this other person as
   doing fine as you are falling on the Via Dolorosa, on the stones
   that are uneven, hard, and cold? In this effect, you might have
   begun to see yourself as less of a person, someone qualitatively
   beneath the one who hurt you. Yet, Jesus sees you as someone who has inestimable, loving worth. After all, Jesus went
   through His suffering for you.

7. An effect that is quite difficult to bear is this: Has the injustice
   led to your changing life plans, to change what you did not
   want to change? Keep in mind that Jesus left heaven to enter
   the fallen world, a sinful world filled with confusion, pain, and
   even evil. You share this kind of change with Him. He was
   born as an infant, not even in a luxury hotel but instead in a
   lowly stable with the animals. You share change with Jesus.

8. A final effect upon which we will reflect is your philosophy
   of life, your worldview. Have you by any chance drifted into
   a worldview that is more negative than it used to be? Is there
   anything that is negative inside of you that is an effect of this
   injustice? Has your anger or disappointment or frustration
   come out on others in your community? Have you become
   angry with God, asking how He could allow your suffering?
   Has your theology changed at all? Is it still orthodox and true
   to the Church? Sometimes our wounds can lead to unclear
   thinking. Of course, we can reverse this, but we first have to
   acknowledge this.

9. I am sure there are other effects of the injustice, but we have examined some of the important ones. You share some of these with Jesus Himself. Thus, even in your pain of this world, Jesus experienced much of this as you have. Of course, He never changed His worldview, but He certainly suffered injustices and the effects of them, including death on a Cross. Please keep in mind, as you continue to explore the effects that have come to visit you, that you are human and it is all right to experience the pains from the injustices of others.

GUIDED PRIVATE REFLECTION WITH REDEMPTIVE SUFFERING AS THE FOUNDATION: DECISION AND WORK PHASES

LET US NOW MOVE to the Decision Phase and continue with your journal reflections. Do you actually want to forgive the person deeply from your heart? Do you want to complete what is lacking in the afflictions of Jesus Christ for His sake and then aid the one who had you take up your Cross? Do you want to unite with Jesus in His suffering for the one who made you suffer?

1. You will not be excusing what the person did. The injustice against you was wrong, is wrong, and always will be wrong. You may or may not reconcile with the person. I think our Heavenly Father would want all of us reconciled and be one with Him but the other who hurt you has to say "yes" to this. When you are on the Cross with Jesus, please keep in mind that His Cross work is an act of perfect justice and perfect mercy. He thus is fighting for what is just and so would you be doing on the Cross. Yours is not an act only of forgiveness. It also is an act of justice with Jesus. Do you want to say yes to this? Again, you can start small, even though it is big in the sense of where we are heading on this pathway, to commit to doing no harm to this person ever again. You will not hurt the

person deliberately. You certainly can talk with others about the person and what happened, as a way to get the burden off of your mind and soul. The point here is to refrain from condemning the person to others. Are you willing to do no harm? Just take a moment to ask yourself: Am I willing to forgive in this way?

2. If you are willing, then let us enter the Work Phase of forgiving. We once again will examine the Personal, Global, and Cosmic Perspectives.

    We start with the Personal Perspective. In Book 1, did you see the person as wounded by others, perhaps when he or she was a child or an adolescent? Here is a new perspective for you: Did Jesus die on the Cross for what that person did to you? Now we are not seeing only a wounded person, as we did in Book 1, but also we are seeing a person for whom Jesus died.

3. Regarding the Global Perspective, did Jesus die for you? It looks to be the case that you share something with the other person: You share a common humanity in that Jesus died for you ... and for me ... and for the other. It may be for different reasons, but it looks like, from our Global Perspective, that we are quite equal with this other person in terms of Jesus' Crosswork. As we reflected in Chapter 4 of Book One, we all are influenced by what the Bible calls "the law of sin" (Romans 7:23–25 and 8:1–2). What does this mean for who the other is? Who is this wounded person for whom Jesus died and who are you for whom Jesus died and who am I for whom Jesus died? We certainly all share this common humanity. We certainly share Jesus' goal for being born in Bethlehem on that Christmas Day for the one who hurt you, and for you, and for me. We all share that.

4. Now let us move to the Cosmic Perspective. Are you in need of the redemption of Jesus Christ? Is the one who hurt you in need of the redemption of Jesus Christ? How do either one of you get to heaven? Is this person redeemable? Are you redeemable? You share much with this person. You both are in need of redemption; you both are redeemable; you are both wounded; Jesus loves both of you; Jesus died for both of you; Jesus wants to be in eternity with both of you, not because of what the person did to you, but in spite of this. In spite of this, Jesus wants the person to be redeemed. Do you want the person to be redeemed?

5. As you see that you share a common need for Jesus Christ, that you share a need for His redemptive work, that you share the possibility of eternal life together, what does this do for your heart? Is it stoney cold toward the one who hurt you? Is your heart getting a little softer as you see that you both are in need of what Jesus Christ did on the Via Dolorosa, on Calvary, in the tomb that was to become empty?

6. Now we move to accepting the pain. Let us go to Mount Calvary. We walk through the stone courtyard and enter the large door of the Church of the Holy Sepulcher in Jerusalem. Immediately to our right are some very steep, Medieval-type stairs. Let us climb up those stairs now. As we enter the room on the second floor, we see there many vases hanging from the ceiling. Let us go around to the right and there is Mount Calvary. Do you see the large white stone exposed under glass to the right of the Cross? This formed the Place of the Skull or Golgotha. I want you to see Jesus on the Cross. I simply want you to stand at the foot of the Cross and see Jesus dying for you. He is shedding a lot of blood. Thank You, Lord Jesus

Christ. The "law of sin" is at war with the "law of God" on this very hill, on Mount Calvary.

7. Now I want you to bring the one who hurt you alongside of you where you are standing together at the foot of the Cross on Mount Calvary. As we saw in Chapter 4 of Book One, part of the "law of God" is for us, by grace, to grow in humility. Jesus' blood is dripping both on you and on the other, together. You are sharing a certain spiritual equality with this person as Jesus looks down on both of you. He is dying for both of you and you are sharing this side-by-side. Try now to bear the pain of what the other did to you as Jesus is bearing the pain now for that person and for you together. Keep that image in your mind. People tell me that it is a powerful image which they do not forget: you and the other at the foot of the Cross, with Jesus' blood dripping on both of you, because you are both sinners and you now are bearing the pain as Jesus is bearing the pain. You are imitating your Lord Jesus Christ. You are imitating Jesus by being at the foot of the Cross and bearing the pain without malice, without pushing the pain back onto the person. You simply are there together.

JOURNAL REFLECTION: Take a moment to reflect on this image. What does it mean for you?

8. Now, I would like you to keep this image, but go up higher. I request now that you not be on the ground at Calvary, but to go up onto the Cross with Jesus. He is bleeding. He is calling out to the Father, "Forgive them for they know not what they do." I want you, literally now, to complete what is lacking in the afflictions of Christ on the Cross. Love Him. Love Him

more deeply than ever before. Feel the love. Experience the love. You are completing His love on the Cross in His time of greatest suffering. You are doing this "with Jesus, for Jesus, and to Jesus" (Mother Teresa, 1985, pg. 97). Just stay with Him. Abide in this suffering love with Him.

9. In His suffering and in your suffering, I request now that you not only complete what is lacking in Jesus Christ's suffering but also now suffer, with Jesus, for the one who hurt you. Feel the nails. Feel the crown of thorns for this person. You now are uniting with Jesus for the other person.

> **JOURNAL REFLECTION:** Bless the person who hurt you. Romans 12:14: "Bless those who persecute you; bless and do not curse them." And what is meant by "bless"? We find that in 1 Peter 3:9: "Do not return evil for evil or reviling for reviling; but on the contrary bless, for to this you have been called, that you may obtain a blessing." In other words, you do not speak ill of the person, but instead wish that person well. What now does blessing the person mean to you in this context on Calvary?

10. Now that you are with Jesus, loving Him and being infinitely loved by Him, as He is dying for the other person and for you, and in your suffering — please be aware of your suffering heart, your suffering mind as united with Jesus, pray for the grace to transform your suffering into love. I request that you, with Jesus, look down upon the person who wounded you. That person still is standing at the foot of the Cross. Let us now pray for the person, which is a directive from Jesus Christ Himself in Matthew 5:44, to "pray for those who persecute you":

11. Lord Jesus Christ, I unite my suffering love with You for the one I am seeing at the foot of the Cross. The person is in need of Your redemption and may benefit from my redemptive suffering as You will it. I willingly suffer for this person, with my love for You, so that this person is saved by Your Crosswork and by Your making a little room for me, as we did with the three-year-old and the sandcastle earlier in this book. As we look down together, I am praying that this person be saved and that my suffering love plays a part in this person entering eternal life with You when it is this person's time. I pray this person turn around from the hurtful behavior. I pray that my redemptive suffering, united with You, now plays a part for this person, in his or her seeing the action as unjust, confessing it as sin if indeed it is sin, being absolved of the sin, and being with You forever. Further, in my suffering I pray for all who have been cruel to others, that they repent, have sufficient prayers from others, and are saved "with Jesus, for Jesus, and to Jesus," in Whose holy name I pray. Amen. (Quotation is from Mother Teresa, 1985, pg. 97.)

12. You have just given yourself as gift to the one who was unfair to you and wounded you. You are gift for this person. You have made a very important move in your life. You have fulfilled Colossians 1:24 as St. Paul has. You have completed what is lacking in the afflictions of Christ for the sake of His body, the Church, and very specifically to draw this person to salvation which is the point of the Church. So, you are cooperating with the mission of the Church in your own redemptive suffering.

13. You have just exercised the moral virtue of forgiveness in its most profound sense. You are giving of yourself, your wounded self, for the salvation of the other person and for

other persons. This is mercy in action. This is love, the ancient Greek word *agape*, in its deepest sense because you are giving that love selflessly through your own pain for the other's good.

14. What is your level of pain right now on the 1-to-10 scale relative to what that number was when we started this spiritual exercise? Try to remember or take a look at that if you wrote it down. 1 is not much pain at all, while a 10 is excruciating pain. Compare the two entries of your pain. See if there is any movement in this. If it has shifted positively, when did the number begin to shift? Was it when you were at the foot of the Cross? Was it when you went up on the Cross at first with Jesus? Was it when you united with Jesus and looked down to the one who hurt you? Was it when you prayed for the person's salvation while you were united in love with Jesus? When did the transformation take place, or did it happen in increments across all of these exercises?

Guided Private Reflection with Redemptive Suffering as the Foundation: Discovery Phase

We now move to the Discovery Phase. Each of the first seven questions can be answered as journal reflections. We end with three more themes for your consideration in your journal.

1. What is the meaning of your suffering which you received from the injustices of other people? The person who hurt you gave you the opportunity to suffer. Notice that I created a sentence that is different from "the person made you suffer." My emphasis was on the word "opportunity." That difference is important. We certainly do not look for suffering, but when it comes, what is the meaning of it for you now? You now know the depth of meaning of suffering. You know what it is about and you know what to do with your suffering. You know that you go to Jesus first because it all starts with Him and then you go to the other person. Link your suffering to love as Pope Saint John Paul II says. In the case of forgiving, first to Jesus and then to the one who hurt you. Your suffering is giving you the opportunity to love Jesus in a way that may be deeper than you ever have experienced. He, then, is giving you the opportunity to love the one who deeply hurt you, whom you might

not have considered lovable. From the Cross of Jesus, does this change your perspective?

2. As a second point, have you seen through this exercise not only your need to unite with Jesus for the other and the other's need to be forgiven but also your own need to be forgiven?

   Reflect for a moment that you are Gift for the one who deeply hurt your heart. Forgiving others often adds the dimension that I need to be forgiven. As we know, Jesus was not on the Cross only for the ones who hurt you and me but also for you and me. Do you see how forgiving and being forgiven become a seamless garment? The image of the one who offended you and you, yourself, at the foot of Jesus' Cross brings this point home to us.

3. As a third point, did you notice that you were not alone at all from the beginning to the end of this exercise? You forgave with Jesus. Forgiving is a community of persons, even with the Trinity of Persons, the Father, the Son, and the Holy Spirit. Why? It is because forgiving on its deepest level is love; God is love; God is a community of Persons. As you are made in the image and likeness of God, you, too, thrive within community, especially when you have this association with the Triune God. Do you see a whole new dimension of forgiving? It is not you in isolation exercising a moral virtue. Instead, it is you *with* Jesus, exercising the moral virtue of love and it becomes forgiveness because it points particularly toward someone who hurt you. Forgiving is love, with the specific difference with all other kinds of love, in that it is directed toward someone who has hurt you.

4. Given your possible new understanding of forgiving others, I have a fourth question for you: What is your purpose in life?

This is different from finding meaning. Meaning is insight while purpose is action. What is your goal or endpoint or what Aristotle calls your Final Cause to your life? Surely it is and has been salvation with Jesus. What is one new purpose you might have for your life on this earth now as a result of seeing forgiving as a community of persons with Jesus Christ, seeing forgiving as a community of *suffering* persons with Him, and seeing forgiving as a community of love in that suffering? Is there one other Final Cause in your life upon earth to which you would like to point, to strive to achieve? What is one concrete action you now can do to exercise the insights here? *Please take some time to reflect on this in your journal.* You certainly do not have to abandon your previous goals in this life. I am asking for a new insight that might be turned into concrete action. Might the new purpose be the binding of heart-wounds which others suffer? Might you find a way to be a healer of others and a healer toward yourself because you deserve this? Be open to what is happening in your interior life. I like to say that our Heavenly Father is a God of surprises. Be open, please, to being surprised by some new purpose in your life on this earth.

5. What is your opinion? Is the Catholic way of forgiving the deepest understanding and practice of forgiving that you have ever seen or experienced? If so, then does it hurt your heart that so many people are turning away from hearing these truths as they head down the mountain, as they leave Mother Church? How can they forgive, then, in this deeply healing way, healing for self and others, when they head down the mountain? How can we meet them as they are half way down the mountain, at the same level as those, millennia ago, who

were at the same elevation on the mountain, but heading up toward the truth? How can we get them to hear this message of forgiving and awaken in them the love of redemptive suffering? How can you be Gift to them?

We now move to our final questions in the Discovery Phase:

6. How is your heart now? You already have given a number to the pain in your heart relative to the one who hurt you. What is that number now relative to the other ratings which you made as you have been reading this book? The number will show you whether or not you still need work toward the particular person whom you considered here. As I said earlier, forgiving takes time. Be of good cheer if the 1-to-10 number still is high. This is typical because the path of forgiveness takes time. Be encouraged because you know this pathway of forgiving, and I urge you to keep on the path until your pain lessens to manageable levels. Our science shows that this can and likely will happen. Be open to God's grace in this, to His gifts for you.

7. What is your new view of who you are as a person? We have focused mostly on the one who hurt you and now it is time to think about you. Jesus did not die in vain for you, but He died out of love for you. You now are suffering in love with Jesus for someone who has wounded you. Who are you? I think you are an amazing, wonderful human being. Do you know why I want you to see this? It is because it is the truth. Sometimes, when we have been deeply wounded by others, we end up not liking ourselves. If this has happened to you, it now is time to challenge this, to struggle against this lie and say with

conviction: I am a person of inestimable worth, of inherent worth. This worth cannot be taken away by others' injustices against me.

Of course, we need to balance our sense of worth with humility because we all need the redemption of Jesus. Therefore, let us continue this reflection with humility. You have been standing in pain for the good of another person. Because of this, who are you? I want you to love yourself. I want you to reintroduce yourself to you so that you know you are redeemable, you know you are lovable, and you know that whatever happened to you does not diminish your personhood in the slightest. You are far more than the wounds against you. If anything, your redemptively suffering in love increases your humanity. You have had the opportunity to increase the depth of your humanity. I wish the world did not work the way it does: When we are beaten down, we tend to believe the lie. Do not believe the lie that you represent diminished humanity. No, you are a child of God who is in union with Jesus out of suffering love. This love is a little taste of the joys of eternal life with Him forever. I would like you to wait in the hope of the taste of the resurrection to this joy which lasts forever. Please take some time to reflect in your journal regarding this following question:

JOURNAL REFLECTION: Who are you as a person?

8. In the future, those dear people whom you might serve, with your new purpose in life, might be sitting with you, their hearts hurting, and they will be saying to themselves, "I am not worth much at all." They will not come right out with this or even be aware of this. Your assisting others in the future may depend on how you view yourself "with Jesus, for Jesus, and to Jesus"

(Mother Teresa, 1985, pg. 97). So, first I would like you to know who you are and please never forget that. You are someone who bears suffering in love with Jesus for others. You now can bring this truth to hurting others, that they, too, when treated unjustly, can forgive people in this deep and beautiful way.

> **JOURNAL REFLECTION:** What does this exercise mean for how you might help people recover from the lie that they are worthless?

9. Also in the future, please keep in mind that those who hurt you might consider themselves as lower than dirt for what was perpetrated onto you. If you can safely be in conversation with any of them, they will need to know the power of the Sacrament of Reconciliation and to know the truth: Each of these persons has built-in worth. Again, if it is safe for you to communicate with the person on whom you have focused in this redemptive suffering and forgiveness exercise, then you might be the bearer of this message to him or her.

> **JOURNAL REFLECTION:** How can you safely bring the message to those who have hurt you that each is redeemable and each has great worth as a person?

10. The paradox of your forgiving others is this: As you are Gift to and for others, you receive gift in the form of grace. You are Gift who receives gift.

> **JOURNAL REFLECTION:** What gifts do you see God giving you when you redemptively suffer in love as you forgive others?

CHAPTER 8

FILLING OUT THE PERSONAL
FORGIVENESS SCALE AGAIN

CONGRATULATIONS. YOU JUST HAVE gone through what I consider to be the deepest, most important way of forgiving someone who hurt you because of an injustice or multiple injustices. The exercise here concerns your current level of forgiveness toward the person whom you have started to forgive in our earlier Guided Private Reflection and the Reflection just completed and on whom you filled out the Personal Forgiveness Scale earlier in this book. Please consider filling out the scale again toward the exact same person and compare your ratings from the past and now. How are you doing from then to now? Recall that you reverse score all of the negatively worded items. Item number 1 is a positively worded item; number 2 is a negatively worded item; number 3 is a positively worded item and so forth. This is for your own private edification as to how you are doing on the forgiveness path.

Personal Forgiveness Scale

We are sometimes unfairly hurt by people, whether in family, friendship, school, work, or other situations. We ask you now to think of someone who has hurt you unfairly and deeply—someone who has wounded your heart. For a few moments, visualize in your mind the events of that interaction. Try to see the person and try to experience what happened.

Now, please answer a series of questions about your current attitude toward this person. We do not want your rating of past attitudes, but your ratings of attitudes right now.

Please rate each item on a 1-to-6 scale as follows:

1 = Strongly Disagree

2 = Disagree

3 = Slightly Disagree

4 = Slightly Agree

5 = Agree

6 = Strongly Agree

For each item, please rate the level of agreement that best describes your current feeling on the above scale. When indicated, place each word or phrase in the blank when answering each item.

This first set of items deals with your *current feelings or emotions right now toward the person.*

I. I feel _____ *toward him/her.*

    (1) warm _____

    (2) negative _____

    (3) kindness _____

    (4) dislike _____

    (5) happy _____

    (6) angry _____

This set of items deals with your *current behavior toward the person.*

II. Regarding this person, I do or would _____.

    (7) show friendship _____

    (8) avoid _____

    (9) aid him/her when in trouble _____

    (10) ignore _____

    (11) do a favor _____

    (12) not speak to him/her _____

This set of items deals with *how you currently think about the person.* Think about the kinds of thoughts that occupy your mind right now regarding this particular person.

III. I think he or she is _____ .

  (13) of good quality _____

  (14) corrupt _____

  (15) a good person _____

IV. Regarding this person, I _____

  (16) disapprove of him/her _____

  (17) wish him/her well _____

  (18) condemn the person _____

Scoring

Now add up your scores as you recorded them for the following items: 1, 3, 5, 7, 9, 11, 13, 15, 17

Important: Now *reverse score the remaining* items: 2, 4, 6, 8, 10, 12, 14, 16, 18. In other words, if you gave a rating of 1, score it as a 6; if you rated an item as a 2, give this a 5; if you rated an item as a 6, then give it a 1; and so on.

Add up your scores on all 18 items.

Interpretation of Your Total Score

If you scored between 18 and 40, you are low in forgiving this person at this point in time. This does not mean that you will not raise your score. If you so choose, you might consider engaging in the forgiveness process to rid yourself of resentment and possibly to improve your relationship (if you have had one with the person).

If you scored between 41 and 63, you are still somewhat low in forgiving, but obviously are getting closer to a psychological state that is not as angry and therefore perhaps not as vulnerable. The midpoint of the scale is 63 and so anything below this shows that you can improve your forgiveness response if you are motivated to enter the forgiveness process.

If you scored between 64 and 86, you are showing forgiveness, at least to a degree. You may have a minimally wounded heart, in need of some forgiveness, but not imperative if you wish to be emotionally free from the effects of others' injustices toward you.

If you scored between 87 and 108, then you are already forgiving or well on your way to even more forgiving toward that person. You probably do not need to go through the forgiveness process further with this person.

> **JOURNAL REFLECTION:** What is your score now relative to your earlier score on the Personal Forgiveness Scale? Do you need to do more work at this point to deepen your forgiveness? If so, what work do you think you need to do?

CHAPTER 9

Questions before Entering the Forgiveness Landscape

1. If someone who offends can come and apologize to the offended, does this quicken the forgiving?

   Yes. Most of us soften our hearts when the other person comes to us in sincerity, with inner remorse, and asks for forgiveness. In some cases, the one who was offended is so angry that he or she is not ready to extend forgiving. This does not necessarily mean that the present unforgiveness is the final word on the matter. In other words, the one who was offended may recall the sincere apology days, weeks, or months from now and that apology may motivate the beginning of the forgiving journey.

2. Is forgiving others unconditional, regardless of the offender's apologizing or not, or is it conditional on the offender's repentance? After all, in Luke 17:4 it seems that we wait until the other apologizes as the Gospel writer instructs: "And if the same person sins against you seven times a day, and turns back to you seven times and says, 'I repent,' you must forgive."

   To answer this question, we have to make a distinction between a necessary condition and a sufficient condition. For a necessary condition, if B is to occur, then it must be preceded, without exception, by A. For water to freeze (B) there must be, without exception, a certain temperature applied to that water (A). For a sufficient condition, if B occurs, it could happen even without A occurring. To make another person happy (B) you do not have to give the other a present (A). Instead, you could smile (another A) or say a kind word (another A) to him or her.

Luke in 17:4 is discussing a sufficient condition and not a necessary condition: If a person comes to you and truly repents, you should forgive. Yet, other Bible passages clearly discuss forgiving without holding out the requirement that the other first repents. Consider, for example, the Lord's Prayer in Matthew 6:5–15. We are exhorted to forgive with no mention of the other's repentance first. This same sense of forgiving, without a mention of the other's repentance, is shown in St. Paul's epistles:

> *Ephesians 4:32: And be kind to one another, tenderhearted, forgiving one another, as God in Christ forgave you.*

There is no mention of a prior apology before the exhortation to forgive.

> *Colossians 3:13: Forbearing one another and, if one has a complaint against another, forgiving each other; as the Lord has forgiven you, so you also must forgive.*

Again, there is no mention of a required repentance by the offending person in this verse.

Unconditional forgiving is of moral importance because it frees you to offer love to the other when you are ready. Unconditional forgiving is of practical importance because sometimes the offending person sees no offense and thus will not apologize. Your unconditional forgiving in this latter context means that you are not held prisoner by emotions of resentment until the other uses certain words.

Yet, it also is clear that when the other truly repents, we are to forgive. Consider the parable of the unforgiving servant in Matthew 18:21–35. A servant, who was forgiven much by his king, refuses to forgive a fellow servant who, owing him only a little, implored mercy. The unforgiving servant was thrown into prison until he now could pay back what he owed to his lord.

If the other person apologizes, this does not mean we are complete forgivers immediately. We can commit to forgiving. True and deep forgiving takes time. After all, we are walking the Via Dolorosa with Jesus as we forgive in the way we are discussing in this book. As a further point, your forgiving need not wait until reconciliation is possible or has occurred. This is the case because sometimes those who offend us might show repentance, but then continue with deeply harmful behaviors. As a reminder, to forgive and to reconcile are not the same.

3. Suppose that a person comes to you and says, "I forgive you for what you did." Yet, you are convinced within your conscience that you did nothing unjust. How should you respond?

Under this circumstance, you as the one being accused of an offense can say, "I am sorry you are upset by what I said (or did)." Notice that you are not saying that you are sorry for your own actions (verbal or behavioral). Instead, you are expressing sorrow for the other's current emotions. If, in the future, you see your actions as having been unjust, you can be open to offering a true apology.

4. Can you forgive a system that is unjust? Can I forgive the
United States government for legalizing slavery?

Yes, I do think that you can forgive those who concretely
have been unjust to you and you can forgive those who instituted the system, even if it was 100 years ago. Institutions
are made up of people and so you can forgive those, whom
you have never met, who have devalued you and others about
whom you care. We can forgive the deceased. We might not be
able to engage in the Personal Perspective, but you can engage
in the Global and Cosmic Perspectives. You can pray for them,
for example. Instead of a person upon whom you focus in the
Guided Private Reflection, you focus on the group, which is
made up of persons. It is abstract and so it may be more difficult to forgive a group, but it is possible and it seems reasonable to me.

JOURNAL REFLECTION: With which of the answers above do
you agree? With which of the answers above do you disagree
and why?

CHAPTER 10

Extending Your Forgiving through the Forgiveness Landscape

1. I now want to introduce you to an exercise that might broaden your vision and practice of forgiving. It comes from my book *The Forgiving Life* and is called the Forgiveness Landscape. This exercise came later in my walk with forgiveness. It was not on my mind when I first started to explore this moral virtue. I came to realize that there is more to forgiveness than forgiving one particular person for one particular act. There is a deeper maturity to forgiveness, a deliberate living forgiving to such an extent that you wipe away all of the resentments in your life from childhood to now. The fruit of this thinking is the Forgiveness Landscape. Here is the exercise: I ask you to prayerfully review your life from early childhood, to childhood, to early adolescence, to adolescence, to early adulthood on up and think about the people who both have been unjust to you and have hurt your heart. When you think you have identified a person, ask yourself this: "Was this truly an injustice or was I looking at it through the eyes of a child and it really was not unfair?" This will help you deal with true injustices rather than misunderstandings.

2. Write down the people in your journal, identifying who this was (is), when it happened, and basically what happened in general without going into great written detail on the specifics of the injustice. This gives you the timeline of your wounds, suffered from others. If a person was verbally insensitive to you 100 times, you need not write down each one of these incidents. Instead, take them as one kind of pattern of injustice against you. Try to be concrete, but use the moral virtue of temperance (avoiding extremes) so that you do not list every little injustice when you have a particular person in mind.

3. Try to do this exercise in particular for people toward whom you still have some unsettledness in your heart. Maybe your father or mother or sibling was unfair to you when you were in elementary school as a child. Perhaps someone bullied you when you were a teenager. Maybe someone criticized you when you were emerging into adulthood, when you were trying to make important decisions in your life.

4. Then rate the degree of your current hurt on a 0-to-10 scale for each person and the injustice as follows:

0 = no hurt or emotional wounds whatsoever

1 = a barely detectable amount of hurt or emotional wounds

2 = extremely mild hurt or emotional wounds

3 = very mild hurt

4 = mild hurt

5 = a medium amount of hurt or emotional wounds

6 = more than a medium amount of hurt or emotional wounds

    7 = an amount of hurt or emotional wounds that ap-
      proaches severe

    8 = a severe amount of hurt or emotional wounds

    9 = a very severe amount of hurt or emotional wounds

    10 = most extreme hurt or emotional wounding possible

5. What you then will have is your life's landscape of hurt, across time and across the people in each time period. Then order these in terms of how you rated your hurt. Those who received the highest number are placed on top of the hierarchy and those with the lowest number of your degree of hurt are placed on the lowest level of this hierarchy, yet you still have an unsettledness in your heart.

6. You now have all of the people who have ever wounded you in your life (at least in your being able to recall this at the present time) ordered in this way. For some people doing this exercise, there are only two people on the list, for others there are 30 on the list. This exercise will vary from person to person.

7. Start at the bottom, with the one toward whom you have the least amount of hurt now. Go through our Process Model of Forgiveness, our road map, with this one person, particularly the redemptive suffering path. Take your time. Take breaks. Reflect in your journal on how you are forgiving and any struggles you are having with the forgiveness process. When you have completed this task with this one person, now go to the next person who is a little higher on your landscape list and repeat the forgiveness journey with that person. Continue up the list until you literally have forgiven everyone in your life who has hurt you. When you finish this exercise, which

could take weeks, you will have climbed the holy mountain of forgiveness and have wiped the slate clean of all of the hurt from all of the injustices from all of the people who, in their own imperfections, have wounded you.

8. Of course, you do not have to have all of the inner discontent all wrapped up with one person before starting with another because, as Aristotle reminds us, we are all imperfect forgivers. We often have some lingering anger or sadness left over and that is all right. If you are wishing the person well, if you can pray for the salvation of the person's soul, if you can honestly say within your heart that you have forgiven the person, then feel free to go up the landscape list to the next person. If you wish, after you complete forgiving any given person, you might consider filling out the Personal Forgiveness Scale for that person to check where you are in terms of the degree to which you are forgiving.

9. Once you reach the highest level of hurt, this particular forgiving may be the most challenging for you. Please keep in mind that you already have walked the forgiveness path with other people. You have been building your forgiveness muscle toward these other people and so you are becoming forgivingly fit. I say this to encourage you to persevere. You are ready to redemptively suffer with Jesus Christ for this person who is on the top of your landscape hierarchy. This can take time, effort, prayer, and grace, but it can be accomplished. Be patient with yourself if you struggle to forgive those high up in your landscape hierarchy. Practice and the grace of God are a powerful and effective combination.

10. This is a growth-producing exercise because it will help you lead The Forgiving Life. It will help you develop a love of the

forgiveness virtue. As Aristotle says, developing a love of the moral virtues is a sign of maturity. Further, as you complete this exercise you will realize that no one, no matter what he or she does against you, will ever defeat you. You know the pathway to forgiving. You have stood in the pains of the past. You can stand in the new pains that might come.

11. Some people will tell you that this is an inappropriate exercise because it re-traumatizes you. You are being asked to go back to something totally forgotten and to open up a wound now that was not there yesterday. Yet, if when recalling the person and the event, you still have emotional pain (for example, that is more than mild, such as in the 6-to-10 range based on the chart which you reviewed as you began constructing your Forgiveness Landscape), this indicates that you have not forgotten it. Instead, it means that you may have psychologically suppressed it in the past (suppression is the pushing away of certain issues from consciousness). It is still there waiting to be cleansed. So, in the recalling of something long hidden from your consciousness, you have an opportunity to finally rid yourself of a subtly lingering resentment that may be playing a part in blocking your happiness, your sense of well-being. You see, suppressed anger can still come out in unexpected ways, such as impatience with others, or displaced anger onto others and we do not even connect this new anger with the old resentment that is still in the heart. There is a substantial difference between the event being put aside now because you forgave the person (even with occasional mild anger left over) and not remembering but still carrying resentment in need of cleansing. We are seeking the spiritual help to be released from subconscious discontent that might even now be playing a part in your relationships with others.

Questions and Answers on the Forgiveness Landscape

12. Suppose we have been hurt by insensitive comments, over
and over, by a family member. Now someone in my new
community or family says something similar. How do I know
if this really is an injustice or just a reaction to the hurts that
happened years ago?

When you do the Forgiveness Landscape and ask yourself, "Is this really an injustice or am I over-reacting?" you actually become more clear about the actual injustices. When
a person does not engage in the Forgiveness Landscape or
practices forgiveness infrequently, then there is a greater
tendency to distort the action, claiming an unfairness when
the other: a) did not intend to do wrong (for example, the
other pulled his bicycle up to the "forgiver's" car, lost control
of the bike, and the bike handle put a scratch on the car door.
The one who wants to forgive is angry that his door is now
scratched. Yes, there is damage, but no intention to cause it);
b) engaged in an action that was not wrong (the would-be
forgiver is jealous that a friend is spending some time with
others); and c) actually engaged in an act of goodness, that
is interpreted as unfair. As an example of (c), one child was
angry with her mother for not fulfilling a promise to go to
the park today. Yet, the mother had to suddenly and unex-
pectedly help her own mother who was unwell that day. The
context suggests benevolence rather than injustice. Forgiving actually brings us closer to the reality of what was and
what was not unjust. The practice of forgiveness does not
make us hypersensitive to hurt, but sharpens our mind to
make right decisions.

13. Suppose I forgive someone and then this person walks through the door and all of a sudden I feel the anger again. Does this mean I did not forgive in the first place?

It does not mean that you had not forgiven. As Aristotle reminds us, none of us is a perfect forgiver. Just seeing someone who has hurt us can reawaken negative feelings. This can happen because we associate the person now with what happened a year ago. Thus, the feelings re-emerge. This is just part of our psychology as human beings. All this means is that you once again start on the forgiveness journey with this particular person in mind. In my experience, people who begin again with the forgiveness process do so more quickly with deeper results. So, be encouraged and persevere in your forgiving when this happens.

14. What if I feel no gentleness in my heart toward this other?

When this happens, I encourage you to be gentle with yourself. You do not have to be at the end of the forgiveness process when you begin that process. To forgive others who deeply hurt us takes time. I use the words "the journey of forgiveness" for a reason, to show you that you will not be at your final destination immediately. A motivation to forgive is great. Yet, motivations themselves do not complete the process. Please remember that one aspect of this journey is to commit to do no harm to the other. This is part of the Decision Phase. It is a big step and I want you to see its importance for your forgiveness journey. You can be civil to the other and civility definitely can be part of forgiveness because this is very different from turning your back on the person and then you walk out the door. Please give yourself credit for every little step you take on the journey because you are progressing. We now know the essence of forgiving and the endpoint of forgiving: to redemptively suffer, through *agape* love, with Jesus Christ for the other (which is the deepest essence of what forgiving another person is), toward the possibility of contributing, at least in a small way, to that person's redemption and salvation "with Jesus, for Jesus, and to Jesus" (Mother Teresa, 1985, pg. 97) forever (which is the best possible endpoint of forgiving that person). We must be careful not to condemn ourselves if we have not reached that part of the journey yet. Let us see this goal as an adventure toward which we strive, but not as the endpoint that we are reaching every time we start forgiving.

JOURNAL REFLECTION: With which answers above do you agree? With which answers above do you disagree and why?

It is now time to begin thinking of a complementary aspect of forgiveness, that which occurs when we have offended other people. Let us now turn to the process of seeking forgiveness from others.

CHAPTER 11

Seeking Forgiveness with the Guided Private Reflection: Uncovering Phase

As we seek forgiveness from others, let us first go to the Sacrament of Reconciliation/Confession and be forgiven by God for what we did. Then we are ready to approach the one whom we have hurt. Each of the 11 points below can be journal reflections.

1. Think about a time in which you were imperfect, fell short, and let someone down. We now will be going on one pathway that is parallel with the Process Model of Forgiveness, which we used twice earlier in the book when forgiving someone who hurt us. Just as in the forgiving process, we have an Uncovering, Decision, Work, and Discovery Phase. As we did in the process of forgiving, try to think of one person whom you hurt and the issue is not yet resolved in that you have not considered approaching that person yet. Consider the person now as we go through the seeking-forgiveness process.

2. With regard to the Uncovering Phase, the key is guilt. We have to be careful with this. As we know, our consciences can point the way to legitimate guilt in need of cleansing. Yet, I have seen false guilt in people, the intemperate or excessive accusation of the self when you have not done wrong or have done wrong that is far less than you are thinking at the present time.

We do not want to go through the seeking forgiveness process when there is false guilt. For example, you failed to return a phone call today, but it was not urgent. You are now annoyed with yourself because of this. Well, this is not a grave issue; you did not have an intention to hurt another person; the issue is small, especially if you can return the call tomorrow. The key here is to realize that you are being much too hard on yourself. You only want to engage in seeking forgiveness if you have engaged in a legitimate offense in which you have broken God's standard and therefore you have broken your standard. For those suffering from excessive guilt, I ask them to begin accepting themselves with their imperfections.

3. Yet, when God's standard and therefore your own standard is broken, and you have sought forgiveness in the Sacrament of Reconciliation, and when you are ready, it may be time to seek forgiveness from the person toward whom you were unjust. Should you approach the other with an apology? This will depend on whether or not you think the person will benefit from this. In other words, there may be two motivations for going ahead: to reduce your legitimate guilt and to aid in the healing of the other. Feelings of guilt can still remain after the sacrament if you see that the other is hurting.

4. So, in going ahead, here are some questions to make the seeking forgiveness deep. First, do you have remorse or the inner sorrow for what you did to the other? In other words, the goal is the other's healing.

5. A second effect, beyond guilt, that can occur is similar to what we called shame when you were forgiving. This time, the issue is not shame, but feeling ashamed, which is different from guilt. Guilt is my inner conviction that I have broken

a standard. Ashamed, instead, is the sense that I am being judged. It is not necessarily the case that others are talking badly about you, shaming you, but instead that your own inner world is feeling as if others are doing this judging and therefore you want to hide from that. So, you might have both feelings of guilt and feeling ashamed because of the unjust action.

6. A third issue that can happen is denial. Have you not been completely truthful with yourself about how much damage was done? Here is a question that might help with your answer: When others do something similar to you (as you are considering now with regard to your own actions), how hurt are you? Might the one who was the recipient of your injustice have a similar hurt? You can consider this as an estimate of how hurt this other person might be because of your action. Sometimes, perhaps even often, when we are unjust to others, they have more hurt inside of them than we realize. This takes the moral virtue of humility for us to see this clearly. If this is the case, then this can increase our motivation of moving forward with seeking forgiveness from the person.

7. A fourth point is this: Has your guilt affected your well-being, your health? Sometimes guilt can weigh us down. It can make us unhappy, distracted, and tired. This is why we need to go to the Sacrament of Confession and, as Mother Angelica used to say (God rest her soul), "get all cleaned up." Not seeking forgiveness from the other might be wearing you down. If so, please be careful that you are not displacing your inner struggles onto unsuspecting other people.

8. As a fifth question, and as an effect of your unjust actions, has your life changed as a result of your unjust actions? Have you

fallen into a pattern of communication, perhaps being less patient with others, as an example? Have you been avoiding the
person whom you hurt? Has anything changed, but in a way
that you do not want to continue as it currently is?

9. A sixth question is this: Has your worldview changed as an
    effect of the action or perhaps a series of similar actions? For
    example, have you become less merciful, thinking that people
    might deserve your being even a little harsh with them? Have
    you shut out other people's inner world, not seeing their wounds,
    but instead focusing only on their actions that you see in need
    of change?

10. A seventh and very important question is this: Has your sense
    of yourself changed, perhaps by overly condemning yourself?
    Evil wants you to be crushed by what you did, and that is the
    big lie. You are of inestimable worth. Be very careful not to
    overly judge yourself. A distorted view of yourself can be an
    effect of falling short of God's standards. Please take this ques-
    tion seriously: Are you seeing yourself as worth-*less*? I recall
    one talk that I saw by a Catholic exorcist. He was asked: What
    is one serious issue that you see befalling young people today?
    He responded that the one issue that needs to be particularly
    avoided is self-loathing. Self-loathing, or excessive self-criti-
    cism, is a huge problem that he sees and needs to be eradicated.
    After all, if some people feel a sense of self-loathing, then they
    might conclude that they do not deserve to be in the pres-
    ence of God. They might reason that they are not worthy to
    redemptively suffer in love with Jesus Christ. Colossians 1:24
    might be seen as something that is open to others, but not to
    the self. This is a lie that must be resisted.

11. This self-loathing can be an effect of sin. Self-loathing is a big lie, an illusion primarily because it confuses actuality and potentiality. Yes, a current action may be loathsome, but you as a person have potential for growing ever closer in your relationship with Jesus Christ and His Church. Focusing only on the actual and ignoring this potential in you is the big lie. Have you overdone this judgment toward yourself? Are you engaging now, or have you in the past engaged in, self-loathing, in which you see your value as a person, as a Child of God, as much lower than it is in truth? Can you say that you are special, unique, and irreplaceable? Can you say that you have inherent worth?

The above seven effects of breaking God's and your standard can be reduced through the process of seeking forgiveness from God and seeking forgiveness from the other person. We now will focus on the Decision Phase specifically toward one person whom you have hurt.

Seeking Forgiveness with the Guided Private Reflection: Decision and Work Phases

Decision Phase of Seeking Forgiveness

All eight points below can be part of your journal reflections.

1. Realize that it is good to ask for forgiveness, but this requires the moral virtues of courage and humility. To seek forgiveness often includes hesitancy because you are not sure how the one whom you hurt will react. Courage will help you go ahead. Humility helps you realize that, in fact, you have offended God and the other; humility helps you to be ready to accept the other person's gift if that person accepts your request to be forgiven. Humility does not mean that you are lower than other human beings. We do not want to be intemperate about the humility. We are all in need of the mercy of God.

2. I want you to see how the moral virtues work together. In forgiving, a person offers *agape* love and mercy and may ask for justice. In seeking forgiveness, the person exercises courage and humility together in a temperate way. We do not want the virtue of humility to degenerate into the vice of thinking of yourself as lower than others, as unworthy of gifts given to you.

Work Phase of Seeking Forgiveness

3. I first ask you to work on understanding what the other has gone through as a result of your injustice. Try to put yourself in that person's shoes and realize that your own woundedness has been passed to the other, resulting in a wound to him or her. Now we have the situation in which you have wounded another. We have to see how the person is living with the wounds. The person might be living very nobly with them. At times, the person may lash out verbally to you. In this case, you now may have to forgive him or her for that. Do you see how conflict can keep going back and forth and even accelerate? As Gandhi said, if we keep taking an eye for an eye, eventually the whole world will be blind. Try to see the degree to which this person has been wounded and how he or she is carrying those wounds.

4. Next, try to cultivate this idea, that if this seeking forgiveness works out when the other is ready, then be ready to exercise the moral virtue of gratitude: thankfulness to God for making this happen and gratitude toward the other for having mercy on you. The gratitude right now is in the form of a possibility because the other has not forgiven you yet. The humility which you started to cultivate in the Decision Phase can help you to receive the mercy from the other person if and when this comes. The humility helps you to understand that the other is giving you a gift in this forgiving. You have to be ready to receive with gratitude the gift of forgiving from the other. As we learned earlier (in Chapters 2 and 7 of this Book 2), the person may become Gift to you.

5. Then you want to work, if you can, toward the apology, which can take many different forms. For example, you can sit down with the person and, with remorse in your heart, say the words "I am sorry." You can, as another example, sit down and review what happened to see if the other is ready to accept your apology. When you are getting ready to apologize, see if the other needs more time. If this is the case, then please give more time.

6. As you stood in the pain for the other when you forgave, please be ready to once again stand in the pain if the other still is angry. Please give the person time to walk the pathway of forgiving because, as you know, that path is difficult and filled with pain. You even could say that you do not expect the person to forgive you yet. You might say, "I am willing to work on this as you wish. I am sincerely sorry [this is your remorse coming out], and I realize that you are a person with your own timeline on this. I did hurt you and I do not expect that you have this all wrapped up and ready to forgive me now. I am here when you might like to talk." This could go a long way toward the person's forgiving because you are acknowledging the person's pain, that the person has a process of forgiving, and you are bearing that pain rather than going in expecting the other to be completely ready as you are ready.

7. Even though it is the forgiver who gives the gift as part of that moral virtue, you are giving the gift of patience and assisting the person in his or her forgiving process. Your apology might be just what the other needs to deepen and complete the forgiving process.

8. As you engage in this process of seeking forgiveness toward a possible goal of reconciliation, please keep in mind that reconciliation is an added component to this process. We will have more to say about reconciliation in Chapter 14.

CHAPTER 13

Seeking Forgiveness with the Guided Private Reflection: Discovery Phase

Discovery Phase of Seeking Forgiveness

Please consider reflecting in your journal on the points below.

1. First, try to find meaning in your personal failure. Realize that you are not perfect and so you are in need of God's mercy and other people's mercy. You are in need of grace and the Cross of Christ, as are we all. What meaning are you, personally, finding in the failure? Another meaning is this: I realize that I can leave pain in the world. I actually can leave more pain to others than I realized. I can leave wounds and I will try, by the grace of God, not to be a person who wounds others. Even though I have been wounded by others, I will try from now on not to wound others.

2. You also can realize that you are becoming stronger as you grow in courage, humility, and gratitude. You are in the process of growing in moral virtue. We all know that it is hard to approach another person and to say, "I know that I did wrong. I am sorry. Forgive me, please." That takes a strong person. Thus, instead of self-loathing, we can cultivate a sense of self that is becoming stronger and growing in the virtues. As you

are able to make up for your failings, then you must and will go against self-loathing, which is an intemperate and inaccurate understanding of yourself.

3. As in forgiving, within seeking forgiveness we realize that we are not alone. How do we Catholics know that we are not alone? We go to the Sacrament of Reconciliation. Our Heavenly Father is accompanying us in our seeking-forgiveness process. We might even have a confidant who encourages and supports us.

4. I see a particularly important purpose when we combine forgiving and seeking forgiveness. It is this: As we make these decisions to forgive and to amend our ways, we begin to realize that we are *growing in our humanity*. One of the most popular works in the Medieval period was Boethius' (534/1999) book, *Consolation of Philosophy*, in which he says that in every choice we make, we can become more or less human because of our free will. The philosopher Peter Kreeft (2005), who admires Boethius, said that we are the only living beings on the planet who can decide to become more like our species or less like our species. Each choice you make can lead to a greater humanity, and therefore more holiness, more Christ-likeness, or less like this. As Pope Benedict XVI (Ratzinger, 2007, pg. 335) clarifies, "The new humanity that comes from God is what being a disciple of Jesus Christ is all about."

5. The squirrels and birds cannot make a decision to become more squirrel-like or more bird-like. They are what they are by their nature. Because of our free will, we are more flexible and so can choose to be more or less *fully* human. As we see we have failed, as we decide to change and to aid a person who is trying to forgive us, as we exercise the courage, humility, and

gratitude in this, and as we bear the pain, we have the opportunity to grow more Christ-like. Listen to St. Paul's counsel to us, which again is showing a qualitative shift in who we are: "Therefore, if any one is in Christ, he is a new creation; the old has passed away, behold, the new has come" (2 Corinthians 5:17). And how does this qualitative transformation take place? Does it occur as we follow our own path or does it occur as we deliberately choose Christ? As the writer exhorts us in Romans 13:14 we are to "put on the Lord Jesus Christ." And what is one way we can choose Him and unite with Him in love? It is through our redemptive suffering (Colossians 1:24) that can be accomplished as we forgive on its deepest level.

6. I think this thought that we can grow or diminish in our humanity is a very unpopular idea in secular culture. It is so because it is considered to be judgmental, to think that you can become more or less human. "We are all equal" is the typical statement. Yes, we are all equal in terms of our rights and our inherent worth, but are we all equal in our exercise of and perfection in the moral virtues and in our growth to become more Christ-like? Are we all equal when some deliberately reject Jesus Christ and decide to forge their own path in life? That is where the unpopularity centers, in the idea that one's own path is any less than the path of Christ. I think that the philosophers Boethius and Kreeft have an important point. Our free will opens the door for us to grow in our humanity or to lessen it. The idea of lessening one's humanity is biblical as we read in St. Paul's second letter to Timothy (3:1–5). In the last days, as he explains, there will be stress because people will exhibit 19 different negative characteristics (such as being lovers of self, arrogant, ungrateful, and haters of good). One of those characteristics is "inhuman." St. Paul (2 Corinthians 5:17) certainly

is right in that God's grace can transform us to be more Christ-like. It seems to me that in our saying yes to the pathways of forgiving and seeking forgiveness, we can grow in our humanity. It is then that we experience true freedom, the freedom to love more deeply and to be a blessing to others. After all, freedom is becoming more of what we truly are designed to be if we so choose that. Forgiving and seeking forgiveness are very Boethian. Forgiving and seeking forgiveness are very biblical in helping us put on Christ and become a new creation.

7. The central point of our reflections across the chapters of these first two books is to grow in our humanity to become more Christ-like. The French philosopher Jean Paul Sartre deliberately rejected faith because he had a distorted view of what freedom is. For him, freedom was the license to do whatever he pleased. He came to what is a logical conclusion, with the wrong premise of what freedom is, that we cannot follow someone else's way for us because it would thwart our own freedom of being made in our own image and likeness. He had the courage to admit that this can lead to despair, but that is just as it must be (see Kreeft, 2019, on this point). Despair, on the one hand, and loving others and the self, on the other, sound incompatible to me. They are incompatible because deliberately living a life that you know leads to despair is to miss the premise that we are all made in the image and likeness of God. Therefore, we are made to grow in love. How do we know this? How do we know that to grow in God's image and likeness is to grow in love? We come full circle back to Book One, Chapter 2 and to our very first exercise, the "Our Loving Heavenly Father" reflection. I urge you to go back to that and quietly re-read it as you reflect on how this exercise connects

to your forgiving, to your seeking forgiveness, and to your growing in your humanity.

8. In summary, as we grow in forgiving, as we grow in seeking forgiveness from others when we are unjust to them, we have the opportunity to grow in love. Being designed to be more Christ-like, as we follow this, we become more free to love and thus we become more human. This is why your understanding and practicing forgiving and seeking forgiveness are so vitally important.

9. As a second purpose here, as we exercise this freedom of choice to forgive and to seek forgiveness, we can deliberately bring these to others, to give them the opportunity to grow in their humanity, to knit back together broken relationships, and therefore to grow in love. What is awaiting them is so amazing that they may not be aware of this right now.

10. Please think about the advantages of forgiving and seeking forgiveness. I have come to realize that God is not a pushover when it comes to our challenges in this life, to our growth as persons. As we move toward eternal bliss, we are in a spiritual battle. God expects us to fight for holiness, by His grace, and the fighting includes suffering. The suffering includes growing and the growing includes loving and the loving includes leaving a better world than before you were born. God wants us to be fighters to overcome our fallen nature and to become holy. Thank you, Missionaries of Charity, for being fighters for others, fighters for their humanity and for their souls. I greatly admire you and those who do similar heroic work.

CHAPTER 14

The Triangle of Forgiveness

When living in community or in a family with others, it is common that people both need to forgive and to seek forgiveness from others. Given that this is a fallen world, we operate imperfectly with those whom we should be honoring with our behavior.

1. It is in this context that we should be aware of what I call the triangle of forgiveness, which includes the deliberate practice in communities and families of: a) forgiving, b) seeking forgiveness, and c) moving toward reconciliation in which mutual trust once again is established. We know a pathway to forgiving and we know a pathway to seeking forgiveness.

2. Yet, the triangle of forgiveness is not as simple as it sounds primarily because the forgiver and the seeker of forgiveness may be on very different points of their respective pathways. For example, suppose one person offended and feels very badly. This person has walked the pathway of seeking forgiveness and is ready to apologize, to make amends, and to reconcile. In contrast, the offended one still is in the Uncovering Phase, is resentful, and not at all ready to receive the words of apology and to forgive. There could be new hurts if the two are not aware of the delicate processes of forgiving and seeking forgiveness. These processes develop toward greater perfection as

people practice them and so those who are just learning them might do so more slowly and with more confusion regarding how to accomplish them.

3. Therefore, each person should ascertain where he or she is on his or her pathway. The two might talk about that first to gain insight into the self and into the o. .er. In the case of number 2 above, the one seeking forgiveness will need patience and humility as this person waits for the forgiver to make progress on that pathway. Both being aware of where the other is on his or her journey should help with the waiting, with the motivation to move forward, and with a genuine reconciliation.

4. Both of you need to realize that each of you has worth and so you are worthy of receiving forgiveness, when the other is ready. Being worthy is not the same as having a right, at this very moment, to the other's gift of forgiving. Why do you not have a right to the other's forgiveness? It is because a right is centered in the moral virtue of justice. Yet, forgiving is centered in mercy and it can take time to offer that mercy, as we saw in the Joseph story in the Old Testament. Everyone is forgivable, but not everyone is ready to offer it at a particular time.

5. There is more on the complications of the triangle of forgiveness. For example, you want to avoid false forms of seeking forgiveness. Please recall our discussion (Book Two, Chapter 9) in which some people are accused of wrongdoing, but they have done nothing wrong. In this circumstance, the accused person might say, "I am sorry that you were hurt by what I did," which is saying in truth that you are sorry that your actions (which you consider to be fair) were seen as unfair by the other.

6. Genuine seeking forgiveness and genuine forgiving can be mutually beneficial. Your seeking forgiving can reduce your own feelings of guilt and, at the same time, assist the other to forgive. Your apology might help the offended person to forgive more deeply and more quickly than otherwise might have been the case. In other words, your seeking forgiveness in a sincere way can help release the other person's challenging effects of the injustice, and, as we have seen, those troubling effects of injustice can last for years in a person's heart. Your forgiving another person can assist him or her in alleviating feelings of guilt that otherwise might have lasted for years in the heart. You are helping each other to get your lives back.

7. Humility plays a part here. If you are seeking forgiveness, prepare your heart, through humility, to be ready to receive the other's gift of forgiving when that person is ready to forgive. Humility counters the vice of pride, the idea that you are owed a great deal even if you behaved badly. Humility can help the forgiver see that both the one who offended and the self have equal worth.

8. Reconciliation is not the same as forgiving or seeking forgiveness. Reconciliation is not a moral virtue. It is a negotiation strategy which occurs when two or more people come together in mutual trust. Reconciliation is one of the goals of forgiving and it can occur beautifully when both parties engage in the journeys of forgiving and seeking forgiveness.

9. When there is deep hurt, then there tends to be mistrust at least by one person for the other. In this circumstance, forgiving and seeking and receiving forgiveness are vital to a genuine reconciliation in which mutual trust is restored.

10. How can we start building trust? How does the one who was hurt know that the injustice will not occur again, especially as a pattern? I refer to The 3 R's which help in completing the triangle of forgiveness: remorse, repentance, and recompense. If the one who acted unjustly has walked the pathway of seeking forgiveness and if the hurt person has walked the pathway of forgiving, then consider The 3 R's. Does the one who acted unjustly show *remorse*, or inner sorrow? Does the person have guilt, and is the person aware that he or she in fact does have this guilt? We usually can tell if someone is faking this because our radar tends to pick up a certain insincerity in others. Does the person seem sincerely sorrowful? Has the one who acted unjustly shown *repentance*, which is using the language of sorrow, such as an apology, and can the offended one see that this comes from a sincere remorse? *Recompense* is making up for the unjust behavior as best as one can under the circumstance. When a person has been verbally insensitive five hundred times, it is hard to see how the person can make up for that, especially given that this is an intangible injury. If the person stole ten dollars and can pay it back, this is an example of a genuine recompense, but, as the prior example shows, this is not always possible. Yet, even with verbal sensitivity, the forgiver can see if the other person now is engaging in more respectful communication. Trust then can begin to build in the relationship.

11. The establishment of trust, even with The 3 R's, can take time because trust usually is earned in little steps at a time when there has been a deep betrayal. So, both, again, will need patience as they try to complete the triangle of forgiveness.

12. When forgiving, seeking forgiveness, and reconciliation all are established, then the triangle of forgiveness has been achieved.

> **JOURNAL REFLECTION:** Where are you in the triangle of forgiveness with someone who is important to you? Are you the forgiver, the one who is seeking forgiveness, or perhaps you are both of these at the same time? What do you need to do to complete this triangle with the other person?

BOOK 3

Skeptical Views, Self-Forgiveness, Resurrection Joy, and Your Legacy

CHAPTER 1

More Questions for Your Consideration

1. **Can I forgive God?**

   No. It is not possible to forgive God, because God can never commit an injustice. Forgiving centers on the other who was unjust to you. God, as perfect, all holy, and all loving, cannot by His nature be unjust. Therefore, I think it is flawed theology to think of God as Someone who can engage in injustice. If you are disappointed with certain issues in life, I would recommend that you practice acceptance of what is happening rather than practice forgiving because it is impossible to forgive God Who is perfect. There is a difference between God's absolute will and His permissive will. He allows others to exercise their free will even when they act badly. Yet, others acting badly is not at all part of God's absolute will.

2. **What if I am suffering and therefore angry about that suffering. Can I forgive God for allowing me to suffer?**

   Even though God allows you to suffer, this is not an injustice by God. For one thing, your suffering may help you to grow closer to Jesus Christ, as we discussed earlier. Also, if you become angry over your suffering, I urge you to once again go to the Cross and ask yourself this: "Am I suffering more than Jesus suffered for me?" This may help you to endure your suffering and to accept your current situation as you draw closer to Jesus in your suffering. I would urge you to focus on what is and not ask the "why" question. I say this because we do not necessarily know why we are suffering right now. Sometimes, in looking back to suffering from years before, we now develop new insights into how we have matured because of that suffering, but such insights do not necessarily come right away.

3. How do I know when I actually have forgiven in my heart?

Lewis Smedes in his 1984 book, *Forgive and Forget*, says that we know we have begun forgiving when we wish the other person well. This does not mean that we have to be reconciled to the other (if the person continues hurtful behaviors that just won't quit). One can pray for the other's well-being and for the person's salvation. One can hope that the person is not injured or taken ill today. As you likely will experience, the resentment lessens as you focus on the other living a good life now and, God willing, in eternity.

4. When I forgive, is it best not to have any anger at all, from the very beginning of the forgiving pathway to the end?

The answer is: no. Having sadness or anger is part of the Uncovering Phase. Forgiveness includes the effects of sadness and/or anger. We can make a distinction between healthy and unhealthy anger. Healthy anger is a reasonable short-term reaction to the injustice as you say, even to yourself, "I do not like what the person has done." St. Paul in Ephesians 4:26 tells us to be angry (the Greek here is *orge*) but sin not. He further tells us not to let the sun go down on our anger, and the word for anger here is *par-orgismos*. The prefix *par* and the suffix *ismos* together suggest an intensification of anger, that can include ruminations of revenge. This is what we need to avoid. This unhealthy anger, this *par-orgismos*, is the abiding resentment that suggests ill-will toward the one who was unfair. This form of anger, which is intense, frothing, and revengeful, can stay with a person for years, even for the rest of his or her life. We do not want the sun to go down on this kind of unhealthy anger. Further, we need to have the freedom to be human and people do experience *orge* in the short term when they know that someone has broken the standard of justice.

5. How long until I experience some emotional relief once I begin forgiving a person who has hurt me?

This is a very hard question to answer because it depends on how much experience the forgiver has with the moral virtue of forgiveness, who hurt the person (injustices from loved ones often take longer to forgive because it is the loved ones who should not be acting unjustly toward us), how serious is the injustice, and when this occurred. Did it happen yesterday? If so, the forgiver needs time to deal with the effects of the injustice in the Uncovering Phase. When there is betrayal, the hurt can be deep, requiring a more extended time to forgive. At the same time, people can be more highly motivated to forgive family members because of the goal of keeping intact good relationships within the family. If you keep working on forgiving, you will see a movement in your heart and so please be patient.

6. As a Christian, must I forgive now?

It depends on what you mean by "forgiving now." Does it mean that everything is all wrapped up in the here and now? A key is an intention to forgive. The doorknob of forgiving is the good will that I will start and do my best. Especially when the anger is in the form of *par-orgismos*, it is good to cultivate that motivation of wanting to start the forgiveness journey now.

7. I think that God asks us to forgive only family members and not others. The Bible talks about forgiving one's brother. Joseph forgave his half-brothers and, in the Prodigal Son parable, the father forgave his son. Even the Old Testament shows that most of the conflicts concern sibling rivalry. Do you agree?

     Actually, no. Jesus tells us to love our *enemies* and to pray for *those who persecute you* (Matthew 5:44). We have to be careful not to focus only on those Bible passages that support one's own presuppositions of how the Bible message should be received and communicated.

8. Can you forgive on behalf of other people?

     No. You can forgive on behalf of yourself, but each of us in our free will has to make this decision for ourselves. For example, suppose your brother will not forgive your father. You cannot, on behalf of your brother, forgive your father. Yet, even if the father did nothing harmful to you, you can forgive your father for the hurt you now have because he hurt your brother. The philosopher Trudy Govier (2002) makes the distinction among primary forgiving, secondary forgiving, and tertiary forgiving. Primary forgiving occurs when you forgive those who have directly hurt you. Secondary forgiving occurs when you have pain because of a loved one's pain from another. You can forgive that other for the indirect pain now caused to you as you see your loved one suffering. Tertiary forgiving occurs in a more distant connection, in the case where you know no one who injured or was injured by the action. For example, suppose you strongly disagree with current legislative policies in your country regarding treatment of people who are without homes. If this hurts your heart and even if you never have met the legislators, you can forgive because you see an injustice and it affects you internally.

9. Can we seek forgiveness on behalf of others?

Yes. As an example, Lech Walesa asked forgiveness from the Jewish people of Poland because the government during World War II did not do enough to protect them.

JOURNAL REFLECTION: With which answers above do you agree? With which answers above do you disagree and why?

CHAPTER 2

Skeptical Views of Forgiving

I SHARE THESE VIEWS to strengthen you. As you begin to practice forgiving, some people may come to you with arguments against it. Be ready to share a more positive and truthful view, which may help the critic to rethink the position with the possibility of that critic seeing the moral virtue of forgiveness more accurately.

1. *Forgiving is an act of weakness.* You are caving in to the other's demands and unfairness. This, in other words, makes forgiving an immoral act because it does not stand up to injustice. This view has been around since at least 1887 with Friedrich Nietzsche's book *The Genealogy of Morals*, in which he made claims similar to this. The only reason one forgives is when the forgiver is in a one-down power position and forgives to keep whatever power the forgiver has. Nietzsche's philosophy was based on power. Yet, forgiving in its deepest sense is a self-willed choice to suffer out of love for the other. This is about courage and strength, the exact opposites of weakness and power. When you get on the Cross with Jesus Christ, are you doing so out of weakness or by the grace of God that gives you strength?

2. *When you forgive, you automatically are weakening the offender because you are condemning that person, judging the other as a*

bad person. Forgiveness is a weapon to hurt the offender. Yet, as the philosopher Joanna North (1987) says, we are lowering ourselves in humility so that we are on the same level of humanity as the other. We do not stand above the person, gloating of our power and that person's failures. This lowering the self in humility gives the message that both people have inherent worth.

3. *Forgiveness is alienating to the self.* This is because people naturally seek power in their natures and so the survival of the fittest instinct is thwarted. Yet, forgiveness certainly is part of our true nature of being made in the image and likeness of God so that we love more. Do you see the clash of worldviews here? Those who adhere to the ideology of power think our nature is more aligned with the animal kingdom in which we try to dominate. The Christian view is to work, by the grace of God, to overcome this tendency to dominate, to seek power over others. Forgiveness, then, brings us closer to our true nature as we love as God has loved us. What is the more productive message: "I will defeat you in battle" or "Come, let us join each other in love"?

4. *Forgiving is disrespectful to the other.* If you really respect the offender, you will not forgive so that the other sees the injustice and changes. Yet, cannot you do this work of helping the other to see the moral infraction as you forgive? We must recall that forgiving and seeking justice are compatible moral virtues. They can exist side-by-side. Why must I not be tender-hearted and a justice seeker at the same time? Might your approaching the other in love help the person to be sorrowful for the action and repent? This idea of dichotomizing justice and forgiveness

is a form of philosophical reductionism, seeing the world in an "either-or" way rather than a "both-and" way.

5. *You absolutely must not forgive certain offenses.* Some injustices are so evil that you cannot forgive. The murder of one's child invalidates forgiving, the critic says. Yet, I have never seen any event so horrible that I cannot point to someone who has forgiven. For example, I do know people who have forgiven the murderer of their children. I do know people who have forgiven the Nazis for the Holocaust. The late Eva Mozes Kor is featured in a documentary, *Forgiving Dr. Mengele* (Hercules & Pugh, 2007), in which she states her forgiving of the Nazis. In the film, she is shown in one scene running on a treadmill in a gym. She is robust and enthusiastic about life in her elderly years. She gives the message that it is important to forgive your worst enemies because it sets you free. Her message was controversial because others who were in the Auschwitz concentration camp with her disapproved of her forgiving. Let us learn a lesson from this. Let us not condemn those who by their free-will choice decide to forgive. At the same time, let us not condemn those who by their free-will choice decide not to forgive. We can discuss the beauty of forgiving and even encourage its appropriation, but in the end, it is their choice. Even a person's decision not to forgive is not necessarily the final word on this. By the movement of grace, some people do change their mind and eventually forgive.

These five critiques of forgiveness are some of the battles you will face when you bring forgiveness to others. I want you to be equipped for such battles because it can be rather unsettling when you are doing your best to explain what forgiveness is and another person starts to yell at you. In my own case, I was giving an invited talk to about 100 teachers in a war-torn area of the world. Suddenly, a person near the back of the auditorium stormed up to the podium, snatched the microphone out of the hand of the interpreter, and proceeded to yell at me to stop talking about forgiveness as it is a ploy to accept the enemy's domination. This was about my tenth time speaking in this area of the world and the tenth time in which I had an aggressive attempt to stop the presentation. The person obviously wanted me to crawl under the lectern and stop, but I already had nine other such experiences there. So, I just waited for the person to end the diatribe and I asked this question: Which of the following would you prefer: a) living for the rest of your life without the land that you claim is yours and living with a burning resentment within you for the rest of your life, or b) living for the rest of your life without the land that you claim is yours and living without that burning resentment within you for the rest of your life? The person chose b and let me continue the talk. At lunch, the person still would not make eye contact with me and so I did not completely convince the person of my position, but at least the talk and the important message of forgiveness went on as scheduled.

JOURNAL REFLECTIONS: With which of the answers to the skeptical views do you agree? With which of the answers to the skeptical views do you disagree and why?

CHAPTER 3

Skepticism toward Christianity

1. This deserves its own special chapter. Today there is such hostility toward the Christian faith that I anticipate some people calling for the banishment of this book. Those who will want it banished will have at least the following argument, which I have heard too frequently. The argument concerns Our Heavenly Father and the accusation that He is a child abuser for sending His Son to the Cross. No father, it is argued, would ever do that. An omnipotent Father certainly could and should find a different way to redeem humanity. The wave of His hand might get it done, or perhaps a fiat, "It is now all forgiven," might be considered. Such divine-command-theory approaches fail to see that Our Heavenly Father is the perfection of both mercy and justice. The wave of the hand or even dismissal of sin fails to see God as demonstrating perfect justice, but only indifference if not mercy. Perfect justice requires perfect action. As Turek (2022) argues in her theological treatise, there is biblical evidence, soundly reasoned, that God reveals Himself as perfect *agape* love precisely by sending his Son as the atonement for all of the sins, the injustices, committed by persons. Thus, the Perfectly Sinless Savior has both the perfect justice response to the darkness of injustice as well as the perfect demonstration of merciful love, both combined perfectly on the Cross.

2. For those of you who do not accept this argument in number 1 above, then please consider the following actions (below) that in all likelihood would be labeled as sin. For those of you who do accept the argument, please go to Point 3 below because I want to spare you the mental image of the human horror to be described here: What is the absolutely perfect justice response to a thirty-two-year-old man who killed each of his parents, to obtain the insurance money for himself, and then dismembered them, boiling his mother's head in a pot on the stove? Will a wave of the hand be sufficient? Will the fiat "It is all forgiven" fulfill the absolutely perfect justice response?

Perhaps someone with a materialist philosophy of life might say this about the crime: He likely has a brain lesion or perhaps a profound mental illness such as paranoid schizophrenia and therefore he is not responsible for these actions. Yet, this occurred years ago, in 2016, and he was convicted by a jury of his peers, demonstrating that he was judged competent to stand trial. He is serving a life sentence and no brain lesions have been reported. In other words, he did this from his own free will for his own selfish gain. The person with the materialist philosophy might say that such actions occurred only once by one man and so are exceptionally rare. Yet again, as I write this, a twenty-three-year-old man also judged to be competent to stand trial is in court for the exact same crime of murdering and dismembering his parents. Neither can be explained by a materialist cause, but instead by a cause of free will to harm for the self's advantage. I will spare you other horrendous, almost unimaginable forms of human injustice against other persons. I think this one kind of example should suffice to say that the just response, the payment for sin, must

be enormous, loving, holy, and sinless. This is exactly what
Jesus Christ's Crosswork accomplished.

3. Even if the accusers continue to press the point by falsely saying
   that Our Heavenly Father murdered His Son, we must realize
   that He, the Father, did not nail His Son to the Cross. That was
   perpetrated by those who considered Him to be the enemy.
   Sinful humans nailed Jesus to the Cross. Our Heavenly Father
   allowed it for the expiation of sin, an enormous, loving, holy, and
   sinless response to all of the dark horror perpetrated onto others
   over and over across the centuries. Jesus Christ's sacrifice of love
   was for all of humanity. The horrors described in Point 2 above
   were done for selfish advantage.

4. Still further, the accusers might say that this is an act of
   displaced vengeance by Our Heavenly Father toward humanity and, thus, is unbecoming of a loving God. In other words,
   as the accusation goes, Our Heavenly Father is angry with
   humanity and so He takes this out on His Son. Such an accusation confuses the quest for revenge and the appropriation
   of perfect justice.

5. We further must realize that Jesus Christ made a voluntary,
   free-will decision, out of love, to accept the crucifixion at the
   hands of humanity. We read of this in John 10:18, when Jesus
   says of His life, "I lay it down of my own accord." As the Second
   Person of the Trinity, Jesus made a perfect decision without any
   confusion about what was ahead for Him on this earth. In other
   words, this was not the Father coercing His Son into this.

6. The ultimate response to evil requires heroic love to meet
   that evil head on. As an analogy, suppose you are the head
   of an entire community that is about to be ravaged by evil

forces that have no interest in your community other than to destroy it. You could send your warrior son to the edge of your community because he has the skills to destroy the invaders. You know you will lose your son, otherwise the entire community will be destroyed, wiped out forever. You further know that your son will be miraculously raised from the dead after his heroic act and you will be with him forevermore. Would you send him and if so would this be an extraordinary act of heroic love, the ultimate sacrificial love? If so, how would you respond when those who do not have the eyes to see accuse you of child abuse for sending your son into battle? This analogy is similar to what is happening today. Instead of being eternally grateful for God's ultimate and loving sacrifice, some people accuse Him of unloving, uncourageous child abuse or displaced vengeance against humanity. The lack of insight, gratitude, and love coming forth from the accusers is a sign of darkness and a failure to acknowledge what is needed for the perfect justice and the perfect mercy to save humanity.

7. When heroism and seeing the vital importance of sacrifice are missing from a culture, then such false accusations of child abuse will follow. This, as I hope you see, tells us much more about the comfort-seeking and power-seeking of the accuser than it tells us anything about the Accused.

8. For those who think I exaggerate, let me relate briefly one true story that happened to me recently, as I was writing this book. An accuser wrote to me on Christmas Day, using profanities and stating that he wanted to remove me from the planet because I study and emphasize forgiveness. For him, such an emphasis amounts to a zero-sum game: The more we emphasize the growth in the moral virtues, the less we end up focusing

on technology that could comfort us. I, therefore, am a threat to his comfort and so I am immoral. He still had me on his mind on January 1, on the Solemnity of Mary, a week later. He wrote to me this second time, again using profanity, stating that it would be better if I was eliminated from the planet.

9. Please remember this story when those who think as this man does call for the banishment of the ideas in this book. The argument for such banishment likely will center on how inappropriate it is for me to write a book in which I encourage you to suffer, in a crucified way, and even to do so for those who are cruel to you. It is a clash between comfort-seeking and following one's own path-to-nowhere versus heroic self-sacrifice with the purpose of love and drawing closer to Jesus Christ. In the words of St. Gemma Galgani, "If you really want to love Jesus, first learn to suffer, because suffering teaches you to love" (Kosloski, 2017).

10. Yet, in my presenting the quotation above by St. Galgani, I can hear two other arguments against accepting suffering, especially redemptively for other people. One of those arguments is this: It is unfair to be asked to suffer for another. Why should I have to pay a price now and suffer because other people sinned? As St. Thomas Aquinas instructs, this is an act of mercy that many people have done in paying a monetary debt for those who are destitute: "Since those who differ as to the debt of punishment, may be one in will by the union of love, it happens that one who has not sinned, bears willingly the punishment for another: thus even in human affairs we see take the debts of another upon themselves" (ST I-II: 87.7). In other words, it is not rare for a person of monetary means to assist those who are less fortunate. Redemptive suffering, at least in one of its forms, is the assistance by one person for the direct benefit of another.

11. As a second argument against redemptive suffering, some
claim that such suffering will turn us all into masochists, actually abusing ourselves so that we can help others to salvation.
This confuses our using the suffering, as it comes to us from
the unjust actions of others, for moral good with the vice of
intemperance in which we take the extreme action of trying to
deliberately impose abuse on ourselves. Redemptive suffering
is the opportunity to appropriate suffering for good, linking
it to love, and thus is not a vice of deliberately mistreating
oneself. As a point of clarification, not all suffering just comes
to us. There are instances in which spiritual exercises that
include suffering are willingly chosen. An example is deliberately fasting. Such fasting for moral good is not abuse, but
instead, according to St. Thomas Aquinas (ST II-II: 147.1),
is virtuous, if the fasting is done to "bridle the lusts of the
flesh.... The mind may arise more freely to the contemplation
of heavenly things ... to satisfy for sins." As St. Thomas further
explains in this passage, if a person fasts "immoderately"
(quoting St. Jerome in using this adverb), so as to hinder necessary service to others, then this kind of intemperate fasting
is to be avoided. Thus, such spiritual exercises as fasting in a
temperate way for good purposes are not masochistic abuse
of self or doing harm to others. In fact, St. Vincent de Paul
(International Confederation of St. Vincent de Paul, 2003), in
referring to the challenge of willingly resisting current wants
and needs for a higher purpose, called this a moral virtue:
selflessness or mortification.

12. The ideas in this book are in deep contrast with the appetites of the world, in which mortification is pushed aside.
Dr. Anthony Esolen (2022) says it well this way: "Appetites

are boundless — for sex, vengeance, wealth, rank, fame, and power; but self-denial, humility, forgiveness, and divine worship allay the rage of the appetite and its frustrations, and they raise the mind to higher things, where the old saying really is true, the more the merrier."

13. Two consequences of rejecting the Christian way are: a) purposelessness, with no meaning to life as Jean Paul Sartre, the atheistic French philosopher, admitted, and b) even canceling the messenger, as happened to Jesus Himself and as the suggested antidote to my message of forgiveness, as happened to me on Christmas Day and on the Solemnity of Mary.

14. I find it ironic that those who think forgiveness is abusive, and have the goal of eliminating that abuse, can call for elimination of the messenger. Such twisted logic obviously is not rare. It was applied to Jesus, murdered for bringing the message of divine love. Now it is being applied to Our Heavenly Father, accused of abuse for sending His messenger, His Divine Son, to proclaim that love.

15. We must be very careful not to fall into the secular materialist trap by concluding this: If we accommodate with niceness to the world, then the world always will accommodate to us in return by being nice. This principle of positive reinforcement rarely works when the goal is power over you. As we accommodate to the world, then those of the world, being materialistic, will ask us to accommodate more and more to their power and quest for comfort (the sex, wealth, rank, and fame identified by Dr. Esolen above). It will not be reciprocal mutual respect. Let us, then, live the heroic and self-sacrificial life of love, even if we are accused and persecuted for doing so. The sacrificial love of Jesus Christ is considered to be a sign of contradiction by Cardinal Wojtyła (1979/2021, pp. 15–16) as

he instructs the reader: "May this light give us strength and make us able to accept and to love the whole truth of Christ, to love it all the more as the world all the more contradicts it." Our becoming signs of contradiction like Christ is vital to the mission of the Catholic Church.

16. This contradiction is now to a point that it is at war with the ideas within modernism. This war is explained very clearly by Archbishop Fulton Sheen, who saw this coming as far back as 1931 when he said: "We are engaged now not so much in what might be called a civil war, but we are confronted with what Mr. Belloc has called 'an invasion,' that is, a force of ideas that is as strange to traditional Christianity as Christianity was strange to Paganism. This new invading force is New Paganism. New Paganism may be defined as an outlook on life that holds to the sufficiency of human science without faith, and the sufficiency of human power without grace. In other words, its two tenets are Scientism, which is a deification of the experimental method, and Humanism, which is a glorification of a man who makes God to his own image and likeness. New Paganism is not the same as the old Paganism. The most important differences between the two are these: the old Paganism was a confusion. New Paganism is a divorce."

17. As a final point, I suspect that this rebellion against God, against natural law, and against the traditional moral virtue of forgiveness is grounded in a woundedness that is hidden behind the raucous rebellions. I say this based on some of our Forgiveness Therapy research with men in a maximum-security correctional institution in which we found that about 90% of them suffered grave injustices against them as children or adolescents (Yu et al., 2021). Their fury then came roaring out

onto others. For example, one man in this research, who was deeply abused as a child, was convicted of 30 murders, and he is suspected of 70 other murders. Those who today destroy people and those who are trying to destroy God, with the goal of putting themselves in His place, likely have wounds that we are not seeing, that they themselves do not see or do not want to see. The message of forgiving those who have abused them, and especially the kind of forgiveness that includes redemptive suffering with Jesus Christ for those who have mistreated them, is needed now for those who seek the divorce identified by Archbishop Sheen. It may be an important path for their healing, contrition, and salvation. As I stated above, such a message to them, here too, is vital to the mission of the Catholic Church.

Let us now return to our task of trying to grow in holiness through forgiveness, this time with a focus on self-forgiveness.

CHAPTER 4

SELF-FORGIVENESS: CRITIQUES

1. Self-forgiveness can be controversial because some would say that we cannot forgive our own sins. Yet, forgiving one's own sins is not what we do when we self-forgive. To be forgiven of our sins, we need to enter into the Sacrament of Reconciliation and be forgiven by Jesus Christ, with the Catholic priest as the mediator in this sacrament, acting *in persona Christi.* The priest is not exercising the moral virtue of forgiving toward you in the confessional. Even if you have been unjust to him, absolution within the Sacrament of Reconciliation is not about the priest's journey of forgiving you for hurting him. Instead, it is about God forgiving your sins and this is very different from the priest exercising the moral virtue of forgiving toward you because of some offense you might have committed against him a year ago. Further, St. Thomas Aquinas made room for self-forgiveness (not as an act of forgiving one's own sins) this way: He recognizes a threefold categorization of sin: sins against God, offenses against neighbor, and offenses against self (ST I–II, q. 72, a. 4), which implies that there should be self-forgiveness. "For an offense is not forgiven except by" the one offended (*Summa contra gentiles,* IV, cap. 54).

2. In contrast to this idea of self-forgiveness as the process of forgiving your own sins, when you self-forgive you exercise the

moral virtue of forgiving toward yourself. When you forgive other people, you are forgiving the *person* for the offenses, for the trespasses against you. Every offense against another person or against oneself is also a sin against God, for which only God can grant forgiveness of that sin.

Therefore, when you apply this moral virtue toward yourself, you are offering what? You are committing to doing no harm toward yourself. You are offering respect, kindness, generosity, and to the extent possible today, love toward yourself. Offering love toward yourself is biblical as seen in Galatians 5:14: "For the whole law is fulfilled in one word, 'You shall love your neighbor as yourself.'" As a clarification, this love for self is not some kind of self-absorbed activity in which the self now is preeminent. Instead, as St. Thomas Aquinas explains (ST II–II: 25.11), we love ourselves because God loves us. It is from this position of God's love being preeminent that we now can offer love to our neighbor and to ourselves.

3. Can we really offer the moral virtues toward ourselves? By way of review, what then are the moral virtues? As we saw earlier, the *Catechism of the Catholic Church*, in paragraph 1803, states: "A virtue is an habitual and firm disposition to do the good. It allows the person not only to perform good acts, but to give the best of himself. The virtuous person tends toward the good with all his sensory and spiritual powers; he pursues the good and chooses it in concrete actions."

Take justice, for example. You give your very best to others, including an equal exchange (for example, paying the agreed-upon wage to the carpenter who builds a table for you). You know this is good, you are motivated to be good, and you act in goodness. Can you be just to yourself by giving yourself your best, such as adequate rest and nutrition? Can you be patient with yourself? I think so. Suppose you are not understanding the message in a written document. You can take your time, repeat the reading and thinking, and consulting with others who know more about this document than you know. So, you can be fair, patient, and loving toward yourself. And what is forgiving in its deepest sense toward others? It is loving them. We already have seen that it is biblical to love oneself.

4. Recall the simplified definition of forgiving others: You are loving those who are not loving you. When you self-forgive, you are loving yourself when you think that you are not lovable and do not feel loving toward yourself because you have broken a just standard. Therefore, you are applying love toward yourself, which the Bible tells us we should do.

5. There is more to the controversy of forgiving the self. A colleague of mine, Professor Paul Vitz of Divine Mercy University, and Jennifer Meade (Vitz & Meade, 2011) have written an article in which they argue that self-forgiveness is not possible. Let us examine their views and my counterpoints in this valuable discussion. They have good points for us to consider, but I humbly disagree that self-forgiveness is inappropriate.

6. Their first point is that there are no biblical directives for self-forgiveness. Literally that is true because there is no mention in the Bible of our forgiving ourselves. Yet, as we see above, the Bible does tell us to love ourselves. If we can love ourselves in the context of breaking our own standards, then it does indirectly mention the virtue of self-forgiveness, not as an analogy to exercising a moral virtue, but as a practice of a moral virtue.

7. A second issue is this: They are concerned that in self-forgiving, there is the issue of what they call splitting. You split yourself into the good self and the bad self. That, of course, would be an unhealthy thing to do because you are a whole person and you should not be dividing up yourself into such dichotomous parts. So, in this view, when you self-forgive, you focus on the bad self and forgive that dimension of the self. Since such dichotomizing is not good for us, then let us not self-forgive. Yet, I think there is a philosophical mistake here. We do not say when we forgive other people that we first are dichotomizing, splitting, that person into the halves of a good person and a bad person. Instead, we say that we are forgiving this one person, this whole person, for certain actions performed against us that are unjust. This is a person, who possesses inherent worth and who is made in the image and likeness of God, *who behaved badly*. The judgment is toward the behavior. If you condemn, you are not condemning the person, but instead you are condemning the behavior. As St. Augustine (424) reminds us in his Letter 211, paragraph 11, we are to separate persons from their sins: "with due love for the person and hatred of the sin." We make this distinction, when we forgive another person, between at least the *potentiality* of this person to grow in his or her humanity and the current *actuality* of unfair behavior that could and should change. The philosophical error for self-forgiveness is in assuming that our judgment toward ourselves is on a bad part of who we are as a person rather than on our bad behavior. We can and should judge our behavior as morally wrong while we see our personhood as made in the image and likeness of God and loved by Jesus Christ.

8. The third critique of self-forgiveness is this: Embedded in self-forgiveness is a conflict of interest. You are both the defendant and the judge or jury in this trial against yourself. Since in a court of law you cannot take on both of these roles, then you cannot do so in the judgment of your own wrongdoing. You cannot be both the actor of the injustice and the judge of it. It would be too easy to act as your own judge and say that you will let yourself off this time from this offense. The compulsive gambler might too often legally pardon himself, as an example of how he cannot be the defendant and judge at the same time. Such maneuvers would make it far too easy for the gambler to exonerate the self for the purpose of continuing to engage in the vice of excessive gambling.

Yet, the analogy to a courtroom with self-forgiveness, I think, is a false analogy. Why? It is because self-forgiveness is not about putting yourself on trial but instead is the struggle to once again love yourself, not because of what you did, but in spite of this. Of course, this analysis of jurisprudence is correct in that we cannot be both defendant and judge in a court of law. Yet, forgiving others or forgiving the self never take place in a court of law. The origin of such virtuous practice starts, instead, within the human heart. If a judge in a court of law is the one offended by the defendant, then that judge must recuse himself or herself rather than move forward with the case. Thus, the practice of forgiving others never takes place directly in a court of law. It is the same with self-forgiveness in that you are not putting yourself on trial for the broken standard. Thus, this argument against self-forgiveness involves a false analogy. Further, when you have been offended by another person, and you wish to reconcile, you do pass a certain judgment of what should and should not be done. It is the same with self-forgiveness, which involves a judgment on yourself that you did wrong. We do this all the time through our consciences. The key for how justice fits into self-forgiveness is this: in such judgments of what is wrong, we come to know the action was wrong (through our conscience and/or feedback from trusted other people) and then come up with ideas for not engaging in that behavior again. This issue of self-correction is part of self-forgiveness, but it is not the entire story. The rest of the story is now to love yourself again. As an analogy that I think is closer to self-forgiveness than is the court of law, you basically are extending your hand to yourself and are saying to yourself, "Come up out of that pit. You do not belong down there. I will love you despite those actions, now that I know they are wrong. I will make amends to those whom I have hurt and to myself." The self-loathing, in other words, ends.

9. As another critique of self-forgiving, the argument is that it distorts accurate self-reparation. Again, this is an extension of the court-of-law argument: You will not know what is fair self-reparation because of your conflict of interest. Yet, let us look back at the Triangle of Forgiveness, which we discussed earlier in the book. In working your way back to the one who hurt you, you do make judgments of what is fair for both of you to do as you move forward together. Surely, this can be filled with more self-interest than occurs in a court of law, but we press onward nonetheless. It is the same in self-forgiveness. Our conscience alerts us, as do people who care enough to give us the feedback, and now we have to discern how to move forward. Yes, we need the grace of God to move forward, but we indeed can make progress in knowing how to patch up the rift with another person and how to behave now so as to quiet our conscience.

10. Consider, then, the next critique. Self-forgiveness is an extreme focus on the self, therefore engendering narcissism. This would be the case only if we are not bringing with us the intellectual virtue of wisdom and the moral virtue of temperance, or the deliberate avoidance of extremes. If we focus on ourselves over and over for 24 hours a day, then this critique is correct. Yet, is that what we do when our consciences are bothering us? Usually this is not the case. We make plans to go to the Sacrament of Reconciliation, we make a good Act of Contrition, and we make plans to apologize to those whom we may have hurt by our actions. Here is yet another analogy. Suppose you hurt your knee. Yes, you are aware of this when you make certain movements, but do you sit down and dwell all day and all night on the knee? That would entail the vice of extremism and the failure to appropriate the moral virtue of temperance. It is the same when we break a just standard. We need not, and should not, fall into a morbid obsession toward it, which could lead to the distorted perception of self-loathing. Instead, we need that temperance to put the offense in perspective, formulate a plan of self-forgiveness and reparation toward those whom we have hurt, and make this a part of a balanced life rather than being consumed as if this is life itself. No one who writes positively about self-forgiveness makes the claim that you should devote 10 hours a day to it. You might attend to it at your morning prayer time and again in the evening. If you are temperate and wise, you will not become self-absorbed with self-forgiveness. The critique is centered on intemperate self-forgiveness and not on genuine, balanced self-forgiveness.

11. As a final critique of self-forgiveness, why not simply engage
     in self-acceptance rather than the more complicated issue of
     self-forgiveness? First, I am not convinced that self-forgiveness
     is complicated. Second, why would we settle for something less
     than love? Acceptance can be done with a certain emotional
     neutrality. For example, you might accept a person's political
     views with which you disagree, but you are not enthusiastic
     about those views. Acceptance can include respect but it need
     not include love. Self-forgiveness involves the much deeper
     issue of love and therefore is more challenging and yet offers a
     much deeper self-cleansing than acceptance might be able to do.
     In one of his conferences on healing, Fr. Ripperger (2016) said
     that a major impediment to psychological and spiritual healing
     is not having mercy on oneself. To release oneself from continu-
     ing to hold onto the debt (which in this case is caused by one's
     own misbehavior), he recommends self-forgiveness combined
     with contrition, including, of course, the Sacrament of Recon-
     ciliation. Mother Angelica (2016) of EWTN television also
     gave an assent to self-forgiveness.

12. In summary, when I Iook at the biblical directive to love one's
     neighbor as one loves the self, as I examine the well-meaning
     but philosophically problematic critiques of self-forgiveness,
     when I hear Fr. Ripperger, who has a healing ministry, and
     Mother Angelica talking positively about self-forgiveness, I
     conclude that self-forgiveness is real, it is a moral virtue to-
     ward the self which extends to others as you apologize, and it
     is helpful in assisting people to welcome themselves back into
     the human community.

13. Here is where I agree with Drs. Vitz and Meade: Let us not
     split ourselves into a good person and a bad person; let us not

be intemperate about how awful we are; let us not obsess over and over about what we did. All of this, I think, is correct, but again these are dangers of excessive, intemperate self-forgiveness and are not indictments against self-forgiveness itself. Drs. Vitz and Meade have helped me with these clarifications, but we should not presume that these extreme examples are what self-forgiveness is in its essence.

14. I, therefore, would like to make the claim that there is such a construct as self-forgiveness, and it is worthwhile if we keep the warnings above in mind as we proceed.

JOURNAL REFLECTION: Do you agree or disagree that self-forgiveness is appropriate and worthwhile or not? Why do you say this?

CHAPTER 5

INTRODUCTION TO THE PROCESS OF SELF-FORGIVING AND THE UNCOVERING PHASE

1. First of all, you have to realize that you have broken your own internally recognized standard. Guilt, by way of our conscience, has a way of getting our attention. Some people come to me and say, "I know I have broken my own standard. I have received forgiveness from God through the Sacrament of Reconciliation, but I still cannot live with myself." This happens, in my experience of people coming to me, particularly with abortion. There remains a self-loathing. This is where we need self-forgiveness. You see, it is not a substitute for the Sacrament of Reconciliation. Instead, it is a support of it. It is exactly here, when a person is suffering this way, that we do not want to even subtly scold this person by saying, "You have been forgiven by God. Are you greater than God? If not, then accept His forgiveness and go in peace." It just is not that simple. We do not want the person now to say, "Well, what's wrong with me? I indeed have been forgiven by God, but I cannot let this go." We need a way to heal this woman who has had an abortion, and self-forgiveness is the added part of the journey that can complete the emotional healing. It completes the reconnecting with both God and the self. Please reflect on each of the questions below in your journal. My first question

to you is this: Have you broken a standard of justice and need relief from this, even if you have received absolution in the Sacrament of Reconciliation? If so, let us enter the Process of Self-Forgiveness.

Let us now reflect on the Uncovering Phase.

2. As we enter the Uncovering Phase, we go through the list of some possible effects of the injustice to see what the consequences of the sin have done to you. A key and very challenging effect is excessive and abiding feelings of guilt. You are now familiar with our 1-to-10 scale of pain. On a 1-to-10 scale, how much guilt are you feeling in your heart right now?

3. As the second effect, are you obsessing over what you did, thinking over and over about this far too often? What if at this point you are thinking this way: "I should take up my Cross every day and follow in His steps. Therefore, I will live with this obsessing and the internal discomfort." The problem with this kind of thinking is this: There are a sufficient number of Crosses that you will have to bear in life. You do not have to deliberately keep one that can be healed. As an analogy, suppose you hurt your knee and it needs minor surgery to stop the pain. Do you deliberately avoid the surgery so that you can deliberately suffer? I say no. Heal where you can heal and take up your Cross in the other myriad ways in which pain will come to you. We do not seek the pain, and it seems to me that deliberately avoiding healing is an intemperate approach to taking up one's Cross. Let us heal where we can. Forgiveness is a gift from God. Let us accept His gifts of receiving forgiveness and giving forgiveness, even to ourselves. Self-forgiveness can be that added boost to get your life back and be productive in Jesus Christ's vineyard.

4. As a third effect, have excessive and abiding feelings of guilt changed your worldview, your philosophy of what the goals of life are, your view of who people are as persons? Have you drifted into thoughts that you are a terrible person? Have you drifted into the idea that you are so terrible that you do not deserve heaven? This is a big lie from evil and must be resisted. Self-forgiving can reverse a negative worldview and a negative view of yourself in relationship with Jesus Christ.

CHAPTER 6

Self-Forgiveness Decision and Work Phases

As you have done with the Decision and Work Phases in the other forgiveness exercises in this book, please reflect on each question in your journal.

1. Can you now see why the exorcist whom I mentioned earlier sees self-loathing as so sinister? The evil one wants you to suffer from unnecessary and severe feelings of guilt, to obsess over and over about what you did, and to finally conclude that you are irredeemable and unworthy of eternal life with Jesus Christ. In conjunction with the sacraments of the Catholic Church, self-forgiveness can contribute to your release from such feelings of guilt and negative thoughts.

2. Would you like to make a decision to self-forgive? If you say you are not worthy of this, then we need to go back to those effects above and ask: Do you want to seek the peace of Christ, that is available to you, or continue to make the error of thinking you are unworthy? Are you convinced that there is such a thing as self-forgiveness or do you accept the critiques that self-forgiveness is impossible? If you see it as impossible, then with which of my rebuttals above do you disagree and why? If you see it as impossible, then how do you explain the Bible verse that you are

to love others as you love yourself? Hasn't the Bible's wisdom given you permission to love yourself, even when you have broken a moral standard?

3. Self-forgiveness, as is the case with forgiving others, is your free will choice. Only if and when you are ready should you enter into the Work Phase of self-forgiveness with me. Please remember that you will not be "letting yourself off the hook." If you already have gone to the Sacrament of Confession, you have received forgiveness from God. This is not "letting yourself off the hook" at all. You are not excusing what you have done, but we will be changing your view of who you are as a person.

Let us now focus on the Work Phase.

4. As we have done in past Guided Private Reflections, we start with thinking exercises. For the Personal Perspective, have you been living with a pattern of woundedness? Have you been walking around with a hidden wound that you have not shared with others, but it is with you daily? Your guilt has led to your being a wounded person. Do you see that this does not make you a bad person? Being wounded and being bad are not the same thing. Have you suffered enough?

5. For the Global Perspective, is any person in this fallen world perfect? As a person, are you perfect? Do you have to live up to perfect standards, given that we all have a fallen nature in need of Jesus Christ's Crosswork? "Be perfect, as your heavenly Father is perfect" (Matthew 5:48) is our *goal*. It is not our *reality right now*. If it were an absolute reality, then why would Jesus (see John 20:19–23) have instituted the Sacrament of Reconciliation?

6. For the Cosmic Perspective, have you been truly forgiven by Jesus? You may need a little time to get used to this truth so that it is clearly established in you. The truth of this tells you that you are loved, with an eternal love by the One Who died for you, Who died even for this one action that has caused you so much guilt and suffering.

7. We then engage in the exercise of bearing the pain. Once you are deeply convinced of Jesus' merciful forgiveness of you, are you willing now to redemptively suffer with Jesus on His Cross for your actions which resulted in the broken standard? Take some time to abide with Jesus, out of love for Him now, in suffering with Him. You might consider offering up your suffering for the salvation of souls or for those who are being too harsh on themselves for breaking their own standards.

8. Once you are strong enough to stand with the pain which you caused to yourself, it is time to give a gift. I recommend that you first give a gift to other people. If you still have not forgiven someone, try that now. What can you offer that person? Perhaps you can offer a smile or a prayer or a kind word. This gift-giving to others then can soften your heart and prepare you for offering a gift to yourself. I suggest offering the gift first to others because, quite frankly, I see that most of us are harder on ourselves than we are on other people. In other words, it is harder to give a gift to ourselves than it is to give it to another person. Please take some time to reflect on your tender heart toward at least one person whom you have forgiven.

9. It now is time to offer that tender heart toward yourself. You know what that tender heart is because you have given it to others. Yes, this may be a struggle and it could take time but

our goal now is the tender heart freely and lavishly given to yourself. Are you ready to give yourself a gift of love, to reconnect with yourself as a person, loved and redeemed by God? Can you give this tender heart to yourself, as you are on the Cross with Jesus and as you suffer for others?

10. Do you see that if a person never has forgiven others, it may be quite difficult to forgive the self because of that tenderhearted moment that is easier to give to others than to the self? Getting in touch with the tender heart gets you ready to give this now to yourself.

When you are ready, please welcome yourself back into the human community.

CHAPTER 7

Self-Forgiveness Discovery Phase and One Added Component

As we reflect on the Discovery Phase, and as we have done before, the questions below can be part of your journal reflections.

1. Have you discovered that you can love yourself despite what you have done? If so, what are you learning about who you are as a person? Recall that I referred earlier to forgiving others as heroic because it takes humility, patience, courage, and love. I think the process of self-forgiving also is heroic, given that it can be even more difficult to forgive the self than it is to forgive others.

2. What are you learning about persons in general? Do you see that many people are walking around with wounds given to them by others, and these are sometimes hard to see as people dress up in their finery and are polite to one another? Now do you also see that so many of these same persons are walking around with self-inflicted emotional and spiritual wounds from what they have done to themselves? Too many, I think, are walking around with a self-condemning attitude that is robbing them of happiness. Too many, I think, are walking around with the false notion that they cannot possibly be loved by God.

3. Has the self-forgiving process motivated you at all to have a
    new or renewed purpose in life? Perhaps it is to help those
    who have wounds from others and from themselves to see that
    they are loved by God and can be loved by the self.

4. You certainly are not alone in self-forgiveness. This is the
    case because self-forgiveness and the forgiveness from God
    go hand in hand. As you seek relief from guilt by going to the
    Sacrament of Reconciliation, you have Jesus Christ Himself,
    through the ministry of the priest acting *in persona Christi*,
    pouring out His mercy on you.

5. As a final point in the Discovery Phase, but not the final point
    in self-forgiveness, please be aware of any relief you are expe-
    riencing internally. Are you sensing that you are being set free
    from excessive guilt or even from self-loathing? If so, my con-
    gratulations to you. You are overcoming in the spiritual battle
    for victory in who you are as a person and who you are "with
    Jesus, for Jesus, and to Jesus" (Mother Teresa, 1985, pg. 97).

The Added Component to Self-Forgiveness

6. Self-forgiveness is not all within yourself only. In all likeli-
    hood, when you offend yourself, you also tend to offend others
    by those actions. Our sins usually go out to others and thus
    are not isolated to us only. Seeking forgiveness from oth-
    ers who were hurt by those actions is a component of self-
    forgiveness. As you welcome yourself back into the human
    community and love yourself again, please consider going to
    those who were offended by those actions and seek forgive-
    ness from them. Please recall an important point from earlier:
    Even though you are ready to receive forgiveness from another
    person, this does not necessarily mean that he or she is ready

to forgive. You will need humility and patience, as we already have discussed. So self-forgiving includes going to God for the remission of your sins and to others to assist them in practicing the moral virtue of forgiving toward you, when you are ready and when they are ready.

Let us now shift our focus once more, this time from examining the self to considering forgiveness in the context of the community.

CHAPTER 8

Forgiveness in Community

1. It is time now to take a broader view of forgiveness by examining it within community. In his book *Mere Christianity*, C.S. Lewis (1952) talks of three approaches to ethics by using an analogy of musicians playing in an orchestra. One part of the musicians' responsibility is for each to be good within oneself, knowing how to play the individual instrument. This is virtue ethics or character ethics and up to this point in our book, the focus has been on growing in the character virtue of forgiving. A second part of the musicians' mission is to know what symphony they are playing. They need a goal. This is a focus on the endpoint or what Aristotle called the Final Cause of one's expression of the virtues. Our goal in forgiveness is to grow closer to Jesus Christ so that we can be with Him forever in eternity and along the way offer mercy toward others (in the hope of contributing to their salvation) and create more peace on this earth. The third part of the musicians' mission is to cooperate so that each one enters the symphony with his or her particular instrument at the right time to produce both harmony and excellence in the music being played. Such cooperation or existing in community is social ethics to which we turn now.

2. First: The cooperation which makes up social ethics can break down when there is injustice by Person A, which engenders anger within and subsequent possible reprisal by Person B, which can lead to resentment from Person A. Persons C and D now are upset by the conflict between Persons A and B and we have a breakdown in the harmony of social ethics within the community. First forgiving those who are unjust can reduce the anger. Mutual forgiving when Person A and B both are hurt by one another can reduce the anger more broadly. Once anger is reduced, this can lessen the desire for excessive recompense (the exaggeration of what justice is, which can occur with excessive anger). This temperance on the part of the aggrieved can lead to wise approaches for restoring a sense of justice between Persons A and B, leading to reconciliation, which can reduce the disruption within Persons C and D. To summarize, excessive anger can distort the quest for fairness, lead to intemperate demands, and disrupt the clear thinking of wisdom. Forgiveness, when employed after social ethics break down, can strengthen the virtues of justice, temperance, and wisdom, making community harmony more likely.

3. Second: As we saw earlier, God is a community of Persons in the Trinity. We are made in the image and likeness of God. Therefore, we are made to be in relationship with God and with those who are made in His image. How important, then, is community?

4. Third: As we did in Book One (Chapter 5, Point 2), please say the Lord's Prayer and focus on the words "our," "we," and "us," given to us by Jesus Christ. What insights do you have about community from this exercise? If we are to be Christ-like, then we need to bring forgiveness into our community. I think it is tragic that forgiveness is off the radar in the vast majority of communities around the world, whether those communities are families, workplaces, schools, or churches. When little children go to school for the first time, they immediately are introduced to the moral virtue of justice: "Get in line, children," "Sit up straight and no talking now," "Johnny, please pay attention." They so rarely are introduced to the added moral virtue of forgiveness. This could happen if people are aware of this omission, have the good will to implement it, the free will to say yes to forgiveness, and the strong will to persevere in planting it more permanently within their communities.

5. Fourth: The *Novus Ordo* text for the dismissal at Mass is: *Ite, missa est.* ("Go, she has been sent." The feminine article could refer to the Church, or the soul, or the Eucharist itself.) We are all challenged to heed the call of the Church to extend the grace beyond the boundaries of the physical church. To what role do you think the Holy Spirit is calling you in this regard? So many people who enter the Church door have broken hearts. Might an emphasis on forgiveness help to heal them and their family? Might those who have shunned the faith, saying, "Well, what's in it for me?" take a deeper look at what is "in it for me" if they saw such healing taking place, through forgiveness groups and talks within Church settings? Where there is hurting there can be healing. This might help those who are skeptical about the faith to grow in the faith, first by

practicing the moral virtue of forgiveness in the way we did in Book 1 here. We probably would not want to start with the deep, redemptive suffering form of forgiving because the skeptic might get scared and run. You see, we have to come alongside those who are wounded and accompany them. First, help them heal their wounds and when they get stronger, introduce them to the truly exciting, challenging and life-giving truth of forgiving as redemptive suffering with Jesus Christ.

6. Fifth: How does the Eucharist deepen our forgiving others? How does the Eucharist prepare us to bring forgiveness to others? As Jesus is broken for us in the Eucharist, we can present ourselves, in union with Him, for those who hurt us. So often our deepest wounds come from family members. We can become eucharist (with a small "e") for our families as we suffer with Jesus at the Consecration for those who have wounded our hearts. What did Pope Saint John Paul II say about redemptive suffering in *Salvifici Doloris*? It is precisely through the Church where this will flower. It is through the Church, then, that we can give this healing to families. Think about bringing this idea of forgiving to religious communities. Those of you in religious communities, such as the Missionaries of Charity, can label part of your mission as forgiveness. You can become a Forgiving Community, among many other identities. If you label the forgiving as a Forgiving Community, this may strength, deepen, and extend an important norm in your community that forgiving has an honored place as part of who you are.

7. Sixth: What is the connection between the Sacrament of Reconciliation/Penance, our forgiving others, and our bringing the idea of forgiving to others?

8. Seventh: As you reflect on the wounds that each parishioner carries in his or her heart because of others' injustice (from family of origin, school while growing up, family relationships, work environment, and many other contexts), does the concept of *the Body of Christ* take on deeper meaning? If so, what is that new meaning for you?

9. Eighth: As you reflect on the potential for each parishioners' redemptive suffering through forgiving of others, does the expression *the Body of Christ* take on deeper meaning? What does "the Body of Christ" mean in the context of redemptive suffering through forgiving others?

10. Ninth: Will true peace ever be achieved in such areas as the Balkans or the Middle East unless some, at some point, engage in redemptive suffering for "the other"? By the grace of God, what is one idea you have that is concrete and specific in bringing about at least a better peace than now is the case?

11. Tenth: In the parable of the seeds, only twenty-five percent of the seeds actually sprouted and bore fruit. Some ways the flame of the Holy Spirit is quenched as you strive to create a forgiving community might be these: a lack of energy, diminished perseverance over time (a huge problem for any group doing anything worthwhile), and/or not appropriating grace in the mission. We must be aware of these stumbling blocks and counter each one. They should be reviewed by the group and by each member of the group. What do you think is the major stumbling block for your group/family in establishing a forgiving community?

CHAPTER 9

Some Specific Examples of What Might Occur in a Forgiving Community

A Forgiving Community within Religious Groups and Families

The central points of such a Forgiving Community are these:

1. We are interested in the development of forgiveness as a virtue and its application, both within the group as a whole and among its members.

2. For group members to grow in their appreciation and practice of forgiveness, they should do their best to establish forgiveness as a positive norm in the group. The group leaders should value the virtue, talk positively about it, and demonstrate it by regularly forgiving and asking for forgiveness within the group.

3. Some members of the group should be taught the virtue of forgiveness for everyone to have an appreciation and practice of it. This could be accomplished through forgiveness programs for children in families or by having outside speakers talk at a religious gathering.

4. If the group members are to become strong enough to pass the virtue of forgiveness on to others, the group leaders must continue to persevere in their teaching and practice of forgiveness.

5. Examples of questions that could be asked in as little as a 10-minute conversation in adult group gatherings or in families are these, and this can take place once a week or once every few weeks, depending on the group:

✠ What does it mean to extend forgiveness? (Reminder: to forgive is not to excuse, to automatically reconcile if the other cannot be trusted, and it is not to abandon justice.)

✠ Who showed you much love and kindness this week?

✠ What was this like for you?

✠ Was anyone particularly mean or unfair to you this week?

✠ What was this like for you?

✠ How does it feel when you forgive?

✠ When you forgive, what thoughts do you have toward the one who behaved unjustly to you?

✠ In forgiving, how do you tend to behave toward this person?

✠ If you are struggling to forgive someone, what might be a first step in forgiving? (Decide to be kind, make a commitment to forgive, and start small to realize that the individual has worth.)

✠ What difficulties do you have in forgiving someone who has treated you cruelly?

✠ Put otherwise, what makes forgiving challenging?

✠ For you, what makes forgiving easy, at least in some cases?

The family or group leaders are reminded that they are not required
to give perfect answers.

> **JOURNAL REFLECTION:** How can you turn your community
> into a Forgiving Community? How can you persevere so that
> this idea stays with your community for many years to come?

The School as Forgiving Community

6. Our group began forgiveness education in Belfast, Northern
    Ireland, in 2002, as a preventive approach to emotional and re-
    lational healing for people in contentious regions of the world.
    Our intent in the short run is to reduce resentment, which can
    build up in children who are faced with continual injustices
    in their immediate environments. Our intent in the long run
    is to equip students with such a deep knowledge and practice
    of forgiveness that they can and will, when they are adults,
    appropriate forgiveness in their homes, places of worship, jobs,
    communities, and even the wider community which includes
    those with whom they are experiencing conflict. It is our
    expectation that such deep knowledge and practice of forgive-
    ness will go far in mending conflicts, even those which have
    been entrenched in communities for centuries.

7. We began with first grade (Primary 3 in Belfast) classrooms
    because from a developmental perspective it is here that
    children begin to think logically, in terms of causes and
    consequences, and simple deductions. We have the classroom
    teacher spend about one hour per week for about twelve or
    more weeks in teaching forgiveness through stories, such
    as Dr. Seuss' (1954) *Horton Hears a Who* in which a kindly

elephant saves an entire village of tiny Whos because, as Horton knows and constantly proclaims throughout the book, "A person's a person, no matter how small."

8. We decided to extend the development of the teacher guides through the end of post-primary school (up to age 18), a fourteen-year project. Perhaps the students who grow into adulthood with forgiveness as a continual companion will develop an ability to dialogue more deeply and effectively with "the other side." Forgiveness, properly understood and practiced by some heroic adults, could change the face of communities that have not known peace for centuries. As His Eminence, Sean Cardinal Brady, has said to me, "Ireland can become a beacon of light to the world through forgiveness education." All available curriculum guides from pre-kindergarten (age 4) through grade 12 (age 17–18) are available at www.internationalforgiveness.com.

We now turn to some practical applications and resources for your future, as you continue to grow in your path of forgiveness.

CHAPTER 10

Practical Applications and Resources for Continued Study

As we wind down the exercises in this book, let us examine some practical applications of forgiveness for you during Eucharistic Adoration and at Holy Mass where you can continue redemptively suffering for those who hurt you. I also will offer some resource for your continued study. These exercises and suggested resources are taken from my talk at the Theology Symposium in Maynooth, Ireland, in June of 2012. The two spiritual exercises are related directly to the understanding of forgiving as being eucharist (again with the lower-case "e") for others.

1. While in prayer in front of the Blessed Sacrament, recall that this is the exact same Jesus who has been sacrificed on the Cross both for the one who hurt you and for you. First meditate on Jesus' profound love to suffer in this way for both of you. Second, abide in the loving union with Jesus. Third, then join your wounds to Jesus' wounds and ask Him to save this person who hurt you. Eventually, over days or weeks or months, the emotional pain in your heart is likely to lessen.

2. When at Mass, particularly when the priest begins the consecration, place your woundedness, received from one particular person for one particular injustice against you, on the altar with Jesus. Abide in the love that you share with Him. You

both share being wounded by people's injustices. As He is broken for you and for the one who hurt you, allow yourself to be broken with Jesus for this person. As you go up to receive Holy Communion, pray for this person. As you take in the Body, Blood, Soul, and Divinity of Jesus, broken for us all, unite your wounds, your suffering, with the crucified Christ for this specific intention: that the one who hurt you is saved by Jesus. When you return to your seat, meditate on the fact that Jesus is now inside of you and that you are now united in love with Jesus. From this position of love, meditate on the fact that both Jesus' wounds and your wounds are efficacious in helping this person.

3. Resources

Three publications which may prove helpful in your spiritual growth as a redemptive sufferer and forgiver are: 1) the book *Suffering with Christ* (1952), by Blessed Dom Columba Marmion; 2) Pope Saint John Paul II's Apostolic Letter *Salvifici Doloris* (1984), which is the soaring exposition on redemptive suffering; and 3) the book *Making Sense Out of Suffering* (1986), by the philosopher Peter Kreeft.

For the final two chapters, I would like you to see that, following Jesus Christ, forgiveness is not centered on suffering as the end in and of itself. After the suffering comes the Resurrection, to joy and to new life. It is the same with you. After the suffering from the injustices against you, after the struggle to forgive, comes a taste of the resurrection for you. Let us examine this now.

CHAPTER 11

The Resurrection Joy of Forgiveness

As you recall, we started this book with a reflection on love, particularly God's love as expressed first in the Old Testament and then in the New Testament. The reflections were comforting and that is how it should be because God's is a secure, comforting, Fatherly love for us. We then moved into Jesus' suffering love for us. We did not start there because our walk with God tends to be developmental. We start with the fundamentals (God is love) and then we move to the much more challenging idea that Jesus out of love for us had to suffer and die for us. Then we went to the startling idea that we, too, are to redemptively suffer with Jesus for others who have acted badly against us. Then we discussed this redemptive suffering for all people who have ever hurt us across our entire lifetime. Still, that is not the end of the story and this is why I ask you to reflect on the ideas below of the Resurrection, of Jesus' rising from the dead and so He is alive forevermore. As we have suffered with Christ, so, too, will we rise in the Resurrection with Him, God willing. As it says in Romans 8:17, if we suffer with Him, we may be glorified with Him. When redeemed, we are promised joy. Let us take a biblical look at what is waiting for us.

1. As you begin to see that your sufferings can be made so much more bearable, your joy will increase. We have drawn closer to Jesus in His suffering, and joy is now His and ours when we

are patient. The forgiveness journey is a process, a journey and this takes time.

> *Hebrews 12:2: Looking to Jesus the pioneer and perfecter of our faith, who for the joy that was set before him endured the cross, despising the shame, and is seated at the right hand of the throne of God.*

2. We now know the *path of life*, which goes through the Passion, Death, and Resurrection of Jesus Christ. This is open to us. Let us take a look at that path which is on the Via Dolorosa, on Calvary, and the Empty Tomb.

> *Psalm 16:11: Thou dost show me the path of life; in thy presence there is fulness of joy, in thy right hand are pleasures evermore.*

3. When we unite with Him, we find the true meaning of love.

> *Psalm 5:11–12: But let all who take refuge in you rejoice. Let them ever sing for joy, and spread your protection over them, that those who love your name may exult in you. For you bless the righteous, O LORD. You cover him with favor as with a shield.*

You see, this journey is not just pain as we unite our suffering with Jesus Christ's suffering. That is only a part of the journey. It is not the final destination of that journey.

4. When we unite with Him in our communities and support one another in prayer, there is joy.

> *Psalm 47:1: Clap your hands, all peoples! Shout to God with loud songs of joy!*

5. When we realize that our hearts are lighter as we carry our Cross with Jesus, it transforms us in a satisfying and joyous way.

> *Psalm 63:5–7: My soul will be satisfied as with fat and rich food, and my mouth will praise you with joyful lips, when I remember you upon my bed, and meditate on you in the watches of the night; for you have been my help, and in the shadow of your wings I will sing for joy.*

There is that theme of joy again.

6. When we realize that we now have a deep new meaning to our lives, we experience joy.

> *Psalm 118:24: This is the day which the LORD has made; let us rejoice and be glad in it.*

7. When we realize that we are growing in love, we have greater joy.

> *1 Peter 1:8–9: Though you have not seen him, you love him. Though you do not now see him, you believe in him and rejoice with joy that is inexpressible and filled with glory, obtaining the outcome of your faith, the salvation of your souls.*

8. The connection between uniting in love with Jesus and then experiencing joy is made directly by Jesus Himself when He instructs the faithful this way: "As the Father has loved me, so have I loved you; abide in my love. If you keep my commandments, you will abide in my love, just as I have kept my Father's commandments and abide in his love. These things I

have spoken to you, that my joy may be in you, and that your joy may be full" (John 15:9–11).

9. Consider St. Teresa of Calcutta's (Mother Teresa, 1985, pg. 42) reflections on joy: "Joy is indeed the fruit of the Holy Spirit and a characteristic mark of the kingdom of God, for God is Joy.... The joy of the Lord is our strength." St. Teresa (Mother Teresa, 1985, pg. 44) then connects this joy directly to her community: "Joy is one of the most essential things in our Society. A Missionary of Charity must be a Missionary of Charity of joy. She must radiate that joy to everyone. By this sign the world will know you are Missionaries of Charity."

10. Let us end with two important Bible verses and then move to our final reflection, this one centered on your legacy.

> *Psalm 126:3: The Lord has done great things for us; we are glad.*

Another great thing God has done for me is to help me understand the path of forgiveness with Jesus Christ.

> *Romans 15:13: Now may the God of hope fill you with all joy and peace in believing, that you may abound in hope by the power of the Holy Spirit.*

If you get discouraged in your forgiving, please remember two themes, first the love that I asked you to cultivate in your heart at the beginning of this book. The love is real. You have experienced it. Also remember Jesus Who fell and asked the Father to please take the cup from Him and out of this came joy forever.

11. So, to summarize, I think that forgiveness is this: We walk
the path of Jesus with Him, to the point of being crucified
in love with Him for the good of the one who was unjust to
us, and we share in the joy of the Resurrection with Him
if we can endure and say yes over and over to His love. You
can get a sense of that Resurrection joy quite literally in
your heart now, which is a foretaste of the eternal joy to
come, which, God willing, will be yours forever and ever.
As St. Paul tells us in Romans 8:18, "I consider that the
sufferings of this present time are not worth comparing
with the glory that is to be revealed to us." Yes, forgiving is
about brokenness and our response to that brokenness, but
also is about joy, the joy of knowing we are loved, that we
have loved, first Jesus, and then those who have not loved
us and we have done so through a broken heart. This transformation from a broken heart to a mended heart, from
suffering to joy, should give all of us great hope in the forgiveness process. As you engage in the forgiveness process,
the hope transforms to an actual experience. You know the
path and you have experienced that transformation within
your own heart. You know the truth of this joy because you
have tasted it.

JOURNAL REFLECTION: What now is joy for you? How can
you possess this joy so that it abides in your heart, even during
the difficult times? What must you do to cultivate this joy?

One sister in the Missionaries of Charity referred to the wounds
as resurrected wounds. Following His Resurrection, Jesus still
could show the Apostles His wounds, but they were scars rather

than the fresh wounds while dying on the Cross. So, as we look back at the exact time of the wounding, we now remember in new ways, with the scars of love rather than with the fresh wounds of confusion or anger.

Let us now end with who you will be at the end of your life.

Your Forgiveness Legacy: What Will You Leave Behind on This Earth When You Pass, God Willing, to Eternal Life?

1. When people use the word *legacy* they often think of physical things, such as leaving a sum of money to others, or leaving a favorite rocking chair to the one who admired it when you were alive. Yet, this is not what I mean by legacy. Instead, I want you to focus on the more abstract idea that you can leave a legacy of anger and resentment and bitterness to others or you can leave a legacy of love, of *agape* love in particular that others can inherit, understand, and appropriate in this world. You are a person who has suffered with Christ for other persons. Those who come after you in this world can become a person similar to this. Your message now in this life could become the words that sink deeply into others' minds, hearts, and souls so that something of you, your message and example of redemptive suffering for others, can be alive and well in others long after you are gone. My challenge to you is this: Strive to leave your love to others as your legacy in this world.

2. It is too easy to leave bitterness as one's own legacy. As I explained to you in Book Three, Chapter 9, I assist with

forgiveness education in zones of the world that have had and are experiencing social conflict. As I related to you in Book One, Chapter 8, too often I see adolescents with angry eyes and I cannot help but ask myself: Did this Child of God, in a social, not a biological sense, inherit such anger? Who was wounded and left this legacy for this Child of God and who wounded the one who wounded the Child of God and who wounded the one who wounded the one who wounded this Child of God? Do you see how bitterness can be passed through generations of communities and families? Yet, and here is the good news, love also can be passed down the generations. I think it takes more of a strong will and lots of perseverance to do this because, sadly, it seems easier to pass anger than to pass love to others. Thus, let us cultivate our strong wills, "with Jesus, for Jesus, and to Jesus" (Mother Teresa, 1985, pg. 97), and, by His grace, persevere in doing good. Let us persevere in our loving redemptive suffering and pass this to others. May your loving redemptive suffering live on long after you are with Jesus, God willing, in your heavenly reward.

3.   Consider the words of the Venerable Servant of God Archbishop Fulton Sheen for you. These come from his 1936 book, *Calvary and the Mass*, pgs. 43 and 44: "Our Lord finished his work, but we have not finished ours. He pointed the way we must follow. He laid down the Cross at the finish, but we must take it up. He finished Redemption in His physical body, but we have not finished it in His Mystical Body. He has finished salvation, we have not yet applied it to our souls. He has finished the Temple, but we must live in it. He has finished the model Cross, we must fashion ours to its pattern. He finished

sowing the seed, we must reap the harvest. ... The Crucifixion was not meant to be an inspirational drama, but a pattern act on which to model our lives. We are not meant to sit and watch the Cross as something done and ended like the life of Socrates. *What was done on Calvary avails for us only in the degree that we repeat it in our own lives*" (Archbishop's italics).

4. St. Teresa of Calcutta (Mother Teresa, 1985, pg. 157) has similar counsel for us as she prays: "Jesus, you have died, you have given everything, your life blood, all. Now it is my turn."

5. And so as we come to the end of the book, we reflect on the beginning of the book: The grace of God is transformative. A broken heart can be transformed to a mended heart when we have been treated badly by others. For this to happen, we have to cooperate with that grace, surrender to that grace so that God can provide all that is needed for healing. A major part of healing is to reawaken or to deepen the love within you. For this healing to happen by grace, we are asked to walk a pathway of forgiveness when others wound our hearts.

6. Have you begun to walk that pathway of forgiveness? Have you begun to love more deeply? Please recall that one goal of this book is to not leave the ideas now that you have come to the end, but to return to the forgiveness pathway again and again when treated unjustly by others and to continue growing in love. It is my hope that you continue contemplating the ideas here until they become part of you and then you give them away to others.

> **JOURNAL REFLECTION:** My final question for you, then, is this: What legacy of love will you leave in this world? Please take some time to reflect on this in your journal.

Please remember that this book is one of your spiritual war manuals against the injustices and discouragements of a fallen world. You can use this manual as a protection for your heart and soul and for your relationships. Even if many other people choose the path of anger as their legacy, in the end, Jesus' love will shine, as we see in the wisdom of Pope Benedict XVI (Ratzinger, 2011, pg. 287): "The triumph of love will be the last word of world history." May your renewed heart, through grace, humility, love, and forgiveness, bring healing to the world and honor to Jesus Christ and His Church.

Postscript. Do you recall the man who contacted me on Christmas Day and on the Solemnity of Mary? As we are exhorted to bless those who curse us (Luke 6:28), I wrote back saying, "God bless you." About a week later, in the morning, my wife and I prayed for him, for his conversion. That same day, in the evening, he wrote to me with an apology. In a subsequent communication he explained, "It was your unwavering compassion and understanding that compelled me to re-think and talk myself down." He is even thinking of returning to church.

References

Aquinas, Saint T. (1259-1265/1961). *Summa contra gentiles* (English translation by Corpus Thomisticum, Fr. Roberto Busa). https://www.corpusthomisticum.org/scg4027.html

Aquinas, Saint T. (1265-1273/1947). *Summa theologiae* (English translation by Fathers of the English Dominican Province). Benziger Bros. https://ccel.org/a/aquinas/summa/home.html

Augustine, Saint (424). Letter 211. *New Advent* (https://www.newadvent.org/fathers/1102211.htm)

Belloc, H. (1938). *The great heresies.* Kindle Edition. Location 2649–50

Benedict XVI, Pope (2005). Homily of His Holiness Benedict XVI, St. Peter's Basilica, Pentecost Sunday, 15 May. Vatican City: Libreria Editrice Vaticana (https://www.vatican.va/content/benedict-xvi/en/homilies/2005/documents/hf_ben-xvi_hom_20050515_priestly-ordination.html)

Benedict XVI, Pope (2006). *God is love: Deus caritas est.* Vatican City: Liberia Editrice Vaticans.

Boethius, A. (534/1999). (V. Watts, translator). *The consolation of philosophy.* New York: Penguin.

Dr. Seuss (1954). *Horton hears a who.* New York: Random House.

Enright, R.D. (2019). *Forgiveness is a choice*. Washington, D.C.: APA Books.

Enright, R.D. (2012a). *The forgiving life*. Washington, D.C.: APA Books.

Enright, R.D. (2012b). Becoming eucharist for one another through forgiving. Theology Symposium, Maynooth, Ireland, June 7.

Enright, R.D. (2015). *8 keys to forgiveness*. New York: Norton.

Enright, R.D., Knutson, J.A., Holter, A.C., Baskin, T., & Knutson, C. (2007). Waging peace through forgiveness in Belfast, Northern Ireland II: Educational programs for mental health improvement of children. *Journal of Research in Education*, Fall, 63–78.

Esolen, A. (2022, January 4). Tradition is no dead thing. *Crisis Magazine* (https://www.crisismagazine.com/2022/tradition-is-no-dead-thing)

Frankl, V. (1946/2000). *Man's search for meaning*. Boston, MA: Beacon Press.

Freedman, S.R., & Enright, R.D. (1996). Forgiveness as an intervention goal with incest survivors. *Journal of Consulting and Clinical Psychology, 64*(5), 983–992.

Gambaro, M.E., Enright, R.D., Baskin, T.A., & Klatt, J. (2008). Can school-based forgiveness counseling improve conduct and academic achievement in academically at-risk adolescents? *Journal of Research in Education, 18*, 16–27.

Ghobari Bonab, B., Khodayarifard, M., Geshnigani, R.H., Khoei, B., Nosrati, F., Song, M. J., & Enright, R. D. (2021). Effectiveness of forgiveness education with adolescents in reducing anger and ethnic prejudice in Iran. *Journal of Educational Psychology, 113*, 846–860.

Govier, T. (2002). *Forgiveness and revenge.* London: Routledge.

Hansen, M.J., Enright. R.D., Baskin, T.W., & Klatt, J. (2009). A palliative care intervention in forgiveness therapy for elderly terminally-ill cancer patients. *Journal of Palliative Care, 25,* 51–60.

Haydock, G. (1811/2018). *Haydock Catholic Bible commentary.* Kindle version, ASIN: B07L3XJX15

Hebl, J. H., & Enright, R. D. (1993). Forgiveness as a psychotherapeutic goal with elderly females. *Psychotherapy, 30,* 658–667.

Hercules, B. & Pugh, C. (2007). *Forgiving Dr. Mengele.* New York: First Run Features.

Holter, A.C., Magnuson, C., Knutson, C., Knutson, J.A., & Enright, R.D. (2008). The forgiving child: The impact of forgiveness education on excessive anger for elementary-aged children in Milwaukee's central city. *Journal of Research in Education, 18,* 82–93.

International Confederation of St. Vincent de Paul (2003). *The rules of the International Confederation of St. Vincent de Paul.* Rome, Italy.

John Paul II, Pope St. (1984). *Salvifici doloris.* Apostolic letter, Vatican City: Libreria Editrice Vaticana.

Kaufmann, M.E. (1984). The courage to forgive. *Israeli Journal of Psychiatry and Related Sciences, 21,* 177–187.

Kempis, T.A., edited by Harold Gardiner (1427/1955). *The imitation of Christ.* Garden City, New York: Image Books.

Kiel, D.V. (1986). I'm learning how to forgive. *Decisions,* February, 12–13.

Kosloski, P. (2017, April 11). 5 inspiring quotes from St. Gemma Galgani on Jesus' Passion. *Aleteia.* https://aleteia.org/2017/04/11/5-inspiring-quotes-from-st-gemma-galgani-on-jesus-passion

Kreeft, P. (1986). *Making sense out of suffering.* Ann Arbor, MI: Servant Books.

Kreeft, P. (2005). *Fated and free.* Trinity Forum Academy, Easton, MD, June 6. Available on https://www.peterkreeft.com/audio/29_lotr_ fated-free.htm

Kreeft, P. (2019). *Socrates meets Sartre.* South Bend, IN: St. Augustine's Press.

Kron, K. (2020). Leaning into grief. *Journey,* September. https://www .hospiceofnorthidaho.org/wp-content/uploads/2020/09/PgByPg _HONI_Sep20.pdf

Lewis, C.S. (1952). *Mere Christianity.* New York: Macmillan.

Lin, W.F., Mack, D., Enright, R.D., Krahn, D., & Baskin, T. (2004). Effects of forgiveness therapy on anger, mood, and vulnerability to substance use among inpatient substance-dependent clients. *Journal of Consulting and Clinical Psychology, 72,* 1114–1121.

Magnuson, C.M., Enright, R.D., Fulmer, B., & Magnuson, K.A. (2009). Waging peace through forgiveness in Belfast, Northern Ireland IV: A parent and child forgiveness program. *Journal of Research in Education, 19,* 57–65.

Marmion, Blessed D.C. (1952). *Suffering with Christ.* Mahwah, NJ: The Newman Press/Paulist Press.

Mother Angelica (2016). How can I free myself from guilt? *Catholic Exchange,* October 20. https://catholicexchange.com/ mother-angelica-free-myself-guilt/

Mother Teresa (St. Teresa of Calcutta) (1985). *Total surrender.* Ann Arbor, MI: Servant Publications.

Mother Teresa (St. Teresa of Calcutta) (2010). *In the heart of the world.* San Francisco: New World Library.

Nietzsche, F. (1887/2009). (Douglas Smith, translator).*The genealogy of morals.* Oxford: Oxford University Press.

North, J. (1987). Wrongdoing and forgiveness. *Philosophy, 62,* 499–508.

Park, J.H., Enright, R.D., Essex, M.J., Zahn-Waxler, C., & Klatt, J.S. (2013). Forgiveness intervention for female South Korean adolescent aggressive victims. *Journal of Applied Developmental Psychology, 20,* 393–402.

Rahman, A., Iftikhar, R., Kim, J., & Enright, R.D. (2018). Pilot study: Evaluating the effectiveness of forgiveness therapy with abused early adolescent females in Pakistan. *Spirituality in Clinical Practice, 5,* 75–87.

Ratzinger, J. (2002). The feeling of things, the contemplation of beauty. Presented to the Communion and Liberation Meeting, Rimini, Italy. Congregation for the Doctrine of the Faith. Vatican City: Liberia Editrice Vaticans.

Ratzinger, J. (2007). *Jesus of Nazareth.* New York: Doubleday.

Ratzinger, J. (2011). *Jesus of Nazareth Part Two, Holy Week: From the entrance into Jerusalem to the Resurrection.* San Francisco: Ignatius Press.

Reed, G., & Enright, R.D. (2006). The effects of forgiveness therapy on depression, anxiety, and post-traumatic stress for women after spousal emotional abuse. *Journal of Consulting and Clinical Psychology, 74,* 920–929.

Ripperger, C., Fr. (2016, April 16). The psychological & spiritual effects of being negative. youtube.com

Sheen, F. J. (1931). *Old errors and new labels.* (Kindle Locations 2954–2961). Staten Island, NY: St. Paul's / Alba House. Kindle Edition.

Sheen, F.J. (1936). *Calvary and the Mass.* London: Catholic Way Publishing. Kindle Edition.

Sheen, F. J. (1943). *Philosophies at war* (Kindle Locations 1710–1713). New York: C. Scribner's Sons. Kindle Edition.

Sheen, F.J. (1952). *The seven last words.* Garden City, NY: Garden City Books.

Simon, Y.R. (1986). *The definition of moral virtue.* New York: Fordham University Press.

Smedes, L. (1984). *Forgive and forget.* New York: HarperCollins Publishers.

Turek, M. (2022). *Atonement: Soundings in biblical, trinitarian, and spiritual theology.* San Francisco: Ignatius Press.

Vitz, P., & Meade, J. (2011). Self-forgiveness in psychology and psychotherapy: A critique. *Journal of Religion and Health, 50,* 248–259.

Waltman, M.A., Russell, D.C., Coyle, C.T., Enright, R.D., Holter, A.C., & Swoboda, C. (2009). The effects of a forgiveness intervention on patients with coronary artery disease. *Psychology and Health, 24,* 11–27.

Wojtyła, K. (1979/2021). *A sign of contradiction.* Providence, RI: Cluny. Kindle Edition.

Yu, L., Gambaro, M., Song, J., Teslik, M., Song, M., Komoski, M.C., Wollner, B., & Enright, R.D. (2021). Forgiveness therapy in a maximum-security correctional institution: A randomized clinical trial. *Clinical Psychology and Psychotherapy.* https://doi.org/10.1002/cpp.2583

About the Author

DR. ROBERT ENRIGHT IS a member of the Catholic Church. He is the founder of the International Forgiveness Institute, a non-profit organization established in 1994 dedicated to disseminating knowledge about forgiveness and peaceful community renewal through forgiveness. He holds the Aristotelian Professorship in Forgiveness Science within the Department of Educational Psychology, University of Wisconsin–Madison, and is a licensed psychologist. He is the first to publish a scientific study on the topic of person-to-person forgiving in 1989. For his innovative work on forgiveness, he received in 2019 the Expanded Reason Award, an international award for the integration of science and philosophy and/or theology from the Universidad Francisco de Vitoria in Madrid, Spain, and the Vatican Foundation Joseph Ratzinger/Benedict XVI, for the book *Forgiveness Therapy*. He received in 2022 what the American Psychological Association calls "psychology's highest awards," the APF Gold Medal Award for Impact in Psychology. For decades, he has focused on the importance of forgiveness within the human heart, families, parishes and other faith communities, schools, workplaces, medical settings, shelters for those without homes, correctional institutions, and world conflict zones.